ATTAINMENT'S

teaching to standards
science

earth • biology • waters • chemistry

GINEVRA COURTADE

BREE JIMENEZ

KATHERINE TRELA

DIANE BROWDER

Teaching to Standards: Science

**By Ginevra Courtade, Bree Jimenez,
Katherine Trela, and Diane Browder**

Editing by Linda Schreiber
Graphic design by Elizabeth Ragsdale
Illustrations by Beverly Potts and Gabe Eltaeb

An Attainment Company Publication
© 2008 Attainment Company, Inc. All rights reserved.
Printed in the United States of America
ISBN: 1-57861-662-X

Attainment Company, Inc.
**P.O. Box 930160
Verona, Wisconsin 53593-0160 USA
1-800-327-4269
www.AttainmentCompany.com**

Contents

About the authors

Ginevra Courtade, Ph.D., is an Assistant Professor of Special Education at West Virginia University. She has conducted research on alternate assessments and academic instruction for students with moderate-to-severe disabilities. Her current research is focused on inclusion of students with severe disabilities in school-wide positive behavior support programs. Ginevra has numerous publications, including journal articles, book chapters, the *Early Literacy Skills Builder, Teaching to Standards: Math,* and *Aligning IEPs to Academic Standards for Students with Moderate-to-Severe Disabilities.*

Bree Jimenez, M.Ed., is a grant research associate with the University of North Carolina at Charlotte, where she is also currently pursuing a Ph.D. in special education. Her focus is on creating general curriculum access for students with significant cognitive disabilities. Bree has experience teaching elementary and secondary students with moderate disabilities. She has authored or coauthored numerous journal articles, a book chapter, and the curriculum *Teaching to Standards: Math.*

Katherine Trela, Ph.D., is a program specialist for Charlotte-Mecklenburg Schools, North Carolina, Programs for Exceptional Children. She is coauthor of several journal articles and a book chapter on teaching academics to students with significant cognitive disabilities. She has over 25 years of experience teaching students with multiple disabilities across school settings in New York State and North Carolina. Katherine's interests and expertise are in the areas of assistive technology, instructional supervision and design, and transition. She is coauthor of *Teaching to Standards: Math.*

Diane Browder, Ph.D., is the Snyder Distinguished Professor and doctoral coordinator of Special Education at the University of North Carolina at Charlotte. Diane's research has focused on the instructional needs of students with low-incidence disabilities. She currently is conducting research on math, science, and early literacy for students with significant cognitive disabilities. Diane has over two decades of research on instructional strategies and currently is a partner in the National Center on Alternate Assessment.

Getting started

OVERVIEW

Teaching to Standards: Science is a research-based science curriculum for middle and high school students (ages 12–21) who have moderate-to-severe developmental disabilities (including intellectual disabilities and autism). The curriculum objectives align with state and national standards based on those established by the National Science Education Standards. The curriculum includes four units of study—Earth (Earth's history), Biology (including microbiology), Waters (Earth's waters), and Chemistry—which address science standards using an inquiry-based approach. Lessons are based on the principles of systematic instruction and provide scripts and suggestions for adapting to accommodate students who are nonverbal, have visual or hearing impairments, or have special physical needs.

Teaching to Standards: Science has these additional features:

- The curriculum itself is evidence-based and part of ongoing research on its effectiveness (see Appendix A).

- It is designed specifically for students who have moderate-to-severe disabilities to learn skills listed in state and national standards for middle and high school science.

- The basis for the curriculum is evidence-based practices for teaching science to this population gleaned from a comprehensive literature review.

- Additional suggestions for extending skills or for creating more learning opportunities in the everyday lives of the students are provided as stories in **ScienceWork.**

- The curriculum can be used as a full-year curriculum or as a resource (model) for selecting content that matches specific state standards.

MATERIALS

Teaching to Standards: Science includes many of the materials you'll need to teach the lessons. A list of materials provided in this curriculum versus those you need to supply is included with the classroom kit, or if you have purchased the introductory kit, the list can be accessed at www.attainmentcompany.com.

Implementation Guide. This teaching manual provides the lesson plans for teaching the curriculum. The lessons are based on the principles of systematic instruction and provide color-coded scripts for you to follow.

Student Response Guide. The Student Response Guide allows all students to actively participate in each inquiry question asked. Students who are able to answer verbally should be encouraged to do so; however, students without verbal communication may point to a response

in the Student Response Guide to indicate their response. If a student is verbal but is not able to generate an appropriate response, the Student Response Guide may be used to give him or her an array of choices to choose from. Students who are presymbolic may not be able to use the response book; however, the Student Response Guide will provide teachers with plausible options for matching science objects with two or three pictures from the guide to build symbolic meaning for science materials.

ScienceWork. Each lesson is paired with a science extension story. These stories provide

additional science content in a way that allows for generalization of the content. New information or a greater depth of scientific knowledge is provided in the stories as well as a new context to see the concept applied. Students are asked to follow along as a teacher or peer reads the story. The picture symbols included help students follow along. Comprehension questions following each story allow students to demonstrate their understanding and generalization of the concept taught within the lesson. ScienceWork also includes Appendix pages, which support activities in the science lessons.

Sight word and picture cards. Twenty sight word cards with 20 corresponding picture cards (40 in all) are

provided. The cards represent the science concept and key terminology of each unit.

Illustration/photo cards. Eight cards with illustrations or photos are provided. The 8½" x 11" cards are used for demonstration of concepts in various units.

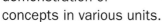

Manipulatives. If you've purchased the classroom kit, materials and equipment needed for the experiments are included, except for food items and items commonly found in a classroom or at home. The storage bin provides extra space for storing materials you gather.

Posters. A 22" x 28" poster is included for use in reviewing the science safety rules. Students should be reminded daily of the safety rules and to treat all materials as "science" materials that are handled with care and caution.

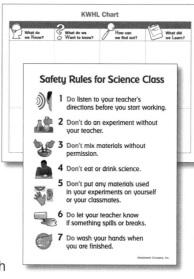

The poster can be displayed in the classroom for all to see. A 22" x 28" KWHL chart is also provided for use in the lessons. This chart has a writable/wipable surface for use with water-soluble markers.

A **Getting Started DVD** is included to give you an overview of the curriculum. The video demonstrations will help you learn the teaching techniques, and you'll be able to view the various experiments. You'll

also observe students using varying response modes, including eyegaze and alternative and augmentative communication (AAC) devices.

A **CD-ROM** containing portable document format (pdf) files of the ScienceWork (SW.pdf) student book, the Student Response Guide (SRG.pdf), this implementation guide (TSS.pdf), and the Table Mats (TM.pdf) are included. Use the pdf files to conveniently print pages, such as the Assessment and Planning Form and the Monitoring Progress Form. An Image Library of symbols used in the program is also included for your use in creating additional materials.

BASIC CONCEPTS

Why teach science?

All students, including those with significant cognitive disabilities, should have the opportunity to gain wonder and understanding of the natural world and their place in it. For this population, it's this outcome of wonder and understanding that will promote quality of life. For example, wonder about the ocean might lead to a lifelong hobby of whale watching or collecting shells. Increased understanding about the human body might lead to choosing to work in healthcare. To gain wonder and understanding, students need to pose questions and share discoveries about the natural world. In science, these abilities are shaped through learning both the process of inquiry and specific science content. In fact, inquiry becomes a tool for learning science content in a way that promotes the desired outcomes of gaining wonder and understanding in ways that are both self-directed (posing questions) and communal (sharing discoveries). Students with significant developmental disabilities should have the opportunity for science learning in an environment that promotes inquiry and information sharing. At specific grades, certain content will be of greater priority as specified in the general curriculum. In setting priorities for alternate achievement, what is most important is to be sure that while students gain some content knowledge, they also are increasing their skills to pose questions and share discoveries, whatever the content of focus.

What is an inquiry-based method?

The National Research Council (NRC) asserts that "inquiry is a set of interrelated processes by which scientists and students pose questions about the natural world and investigate phenomena; in doing so, students acquire knowledge and develop a rich understanding of concepts, principles, models, and theories" (NRC, 1996, p. 214). Within the National Science Education Standards (NSES), inquiry is described as a critical component of a science program. Through inquiry-based instruction, students can learn science in a way that represents how science actually works. Inquiry-based instruction requires more than hands-on activities. Students must follow a problem-solving process that is applicable to the real world. Similarly, students with significant disabilities need instruction that will help them solve problems that occur as part of real-world experiences. Using an inquiry-based approach to teach science to students with significant disabilities allows the students to experience and understand the environments they live in. It also creates the opportunity for access to the same instruction that their general education peers are receiving.

Why use inquiry-based instruction to teach science?

In the vision presented in the National Science Education Standards, inquiry is a step beyond "science as a process" (NRC, 1996, p. 105) in which students learn skills such as observation, inference, and experimentation. The new vision includes the "processes of science" and requires that students combine processes and scientific knowledge as they use scientific reasoning and critical thinking to develop their understanding of science. Engaging students in inquiry helps students develop:

- An understanding of scientific concepts
- An appreciation of "how we know" what we know in science

- An understanding of the nature of science
- The skills necessary to become independent inquirers about the natural world
- The dispositions to use the skills, abilities, and attitudes associated with science

Science as inquiry is basic to science education and is a controlling principle in the ultimate organization and selection of students' activities. The standards on inquiry highlight the ability to conduct inquiry and develop understanding about scientific inquiry. Students at all grade levels and in every domain of science should have the opportunity to use scientific inquiry and develop the ability to think and act in ways associated with inquiry, including asking questions, planning and conducting investigations, using appropriate tools and techniques to gather data, thinking critically and logically about relationships between evidence and explanations, constructing and analyzing alternative explanations, and communicating scientific arguments.

USING THE LESSONS

Unit/lesson description

As mentioned, Teaching to Standards: Science contains four science units. Each unit includes five lessons with a specific concept. The materials needed for each lesson are clearly listed, and how to prepare for the lesson is described. Some materials will need replenishing, and care has been taken to use commonly found materials. Should you need to repurchase an item not commonly found, contact the Attainment Company to purchase.

Each unit includes science terminology that students will need to know. At the beginning of each unit introduce the science vocabulary, and in subsequent lessons, review the science terms. Picture and sight word vocabulary cards are provided for use in teaching the science terms. Following that introduction, a science word wall might be created to build recognition

and comprehension of the science words. Students should learn both the picture symbols and the written word.

Each lesson also includes a list of materials needed and specific instructions, including suggested wording (teacher script) for teaching the lesson. Before reading how to implement a specific lesson, it may be helpful to review some general strategies for inquiry-based instruction. Table 1 on page 9 is an example of the steps in this approach and provides general guidance of how student opportunities are provided as a component of inquiry-based instruction.

Evidence-based practices for teaching science

Teaching to Standards: Science uses effective instructional practices such as systematic instruction along with the inquiry method. In systematic instruction, teachers use consistent prompting with feedback to promote correct responding. The scripts remind you to reinforce students with praise for correct responses and provide correction for errors with simple, informative feedback (e.g., "This one is condensation"). The following are two types of systematic prompting.

System of least prompts. If using the system of least prompts, begin by waiting to see if the student can perform a response with no help. If the student doesn't respond or begins to make an error, give minor assistance (e.g., verbal direction). If the student still doesn't respond correctly, provide more assistance (e.g., model how to make the response). Some students may still not respond correctly and may need hand-over-hand assistance to complete the response. This process is demonstrated in Example 1 on page 10.

Time-delay instruction. Lessons in each unit use a constant time-delay teaching procedure. Use of constant time delay has been shown to increase student learning, both for students receiving the direct instruction and for students observing the instruction in the context of a small group (Doyle, Gast, Wolery, Ault, & Farmer,

Table 1. Steps to an inquiry-based science lesson

Teaching procedure	Opportunities for students
Engage 1. Teacher shows objects, pictures, and/or science materials. 2. Teacher asks, "What is (are) this (these materials)?" 3. Teacher asks, "What do you know (about the materials)?" After students respond, the teacher records answers on the KWHL chart under "K" for "know." 4. Teacher asks, "What do you want to know (about the material)?" After students respond, the teacher records the answers on the KWHL chart under "W" for "want to know."	1. Students make comments and may ask a question about what the materials are. 2. Students respond, using the Student Response Guide if needed. 3. Students identify what they know, using the Student Response Guide if needed. 4. Students identify what they want to know, using the Student Response Guide if needed.
Investigate and describe relationships 5. Teacher asks, "How can we find out?" After the students respond, the teacher records the answers on the KWHL chart under "H" for "how" to find out. 6. Teacher reviews the science safety rules and guides students to make a prediction about the outcome of the experiment. After the students respond to "What do you think will happen?" the teacher records predictions on the KWHL chart. 7. Teacher provides cues to conduct the experiment. 8. Teacher asks students to compare science materials by asking, "What's the same (about the materials)?" 9. Teacher asks students to compare science materials by asking, "What's different (about the materials)?"	5. Students identify how to find out, using the Student Response Guide if needed. 6. Students predict what they think will happen. 7. Students participate in conducting the experiment. 8. Students respond, using the Student Response Guide if needed. 9. Students respond, using the Student Response Guide if needed.
Construct explanation 10. Teacher provides an explanation of the scientific discovery made and ties the science concept to the science vocabulary.	10. Students read or follow along as the teacher reads the scientific discovery statement. Students point to the science vocabulary word and picture related to the science concept and then match the sight word to the picture symbol.
Report 11. Teacher reviews what was discovered by asking, "What did we find out?" and ties cause to effect by asking "Why?" 12. Teacher makes a final summarizing statement about the science concept. After students respond, the teacher records the concept on the KWHL chart under "L" for what was "learned."	11. Students report what they learned specific to the experiment, using the Student Response Guide if needed. 12. Students respond to a fill-in-the-blank statement about the science concept, using the Student Response Guide if needed.

1990). Each lesson begins by teaching or reviewing the vocabulary words for the unit. To use a time-delay procedure, you introduce the target information (e.g., a vocabulary word) with an immediate prompt, meaning you'll point to the correct response as you ask the student to do so. This allows the student to imitate choosing the correct response without making an error. This zero time delay is a warm-up trial. It's followed by another trial, where the student is allowed more time (4 to 5 seconds, if it's needed) to respond before a prompt is provided. This process is demonstrated in Example 2.

After a few days of this process, the zero-delay prompting can be dropped. Show the card and wait up to 4 to 5 seconds for the student to anticipate the correct answer. If the student is correct, give praise. If the student "waits" for your prompt, model pointing to the correct answer and have the student imitate your pointing. If the student guesses incorrectly, use the reminder not to guess, "If you're not sure, wait and I'll help you."

Instructions are given for teaching the science vocabulary picture cards and sight words, using the time-delay procedure in each unit. Remember to include this instruction and review as part of each day's lesson. Table 2 provides a quick reference to the time-delay procedure.

Table 2. Quick reference of time-delay procedure

First days of the unit
Warm-up round: Point to the response as direction is given. The student points to each card.
Delay round: Wait 4–5 seconds for the student to respond. If no response or an incorrect response, model pointing to the answer and have the student point.
Remaining days until the unit ends
Skip the warm-up.
Delay round: Wait 4–5 seconds for the student to respond. If no response or an incorrect response, model pointing to the answer and have the student point.

How often to teach

Depending on a state's standards, some teachers may choose to teach this entire curriculum (all units) during the school year as the primary science instruction. During the pilot of this curriculum, teachers found that the units took most of a school year to complete for students with autism and moderate-to-severe intellectual disabilities. Other teachers may select specific content, because it matches well with their state standards for the grade level, and omit other sections that do not match. The curriculum is not intended to address all standards of all grade levels (a feat that would go beyond science textbooks!), but instead illustrates how to teach to science content at the upper grades.

Teaching to Standards: Science lessons can be taught with the same frequency as a general science program, that is, 3–4 times per week. Lessons generally take 30 to 40 minutes. Typically, lessons will need to be taught several times for consistent student responding. It's important to make sure that most students in a science group have made a connection between the experiment, the vocabulary, and the concept statement. Repetition of lessons will be needed to allow students to gain this connection. Each lesson may need to be taught 2–3 times. During one week, one or two lessons should be taught with some repetition of lessons. It may be possible to build generalization and deeper meaning to science concepts by adding additional experiments from general education curriculum, websites, or science textbooks on a given topic. Each unit will take 4–6 weeks of instruction.

Using Teaching to Standards: Science with full inclusion

Teaching to Standards: Science lessons can be taught in special education settings in a small group instructional format or one-on-one with individual students. When teaching small groups, it's important to provide opportunities for all students in the small group to respond to all questions, as well as to initiate responses.

The lessons can also be taught in general education classrooms. Because the inquiry lessons take a hands-on approach to learning, all lessons can follow the same task analysis to ask students questions in any classroom environment. Individual students or cooperative learning groups can use the KWHL chart to record answers for a given experiment. Students may have selected vocabulary embedded into lessons for repeated practice. Lessons may provide review for students who have already mastered the concept; however, the inquiry format used to teach each lesson can be applied to new concepts.

Providing support for sensory and physical impairments

In teaching the science lessons, it's important that all students have access to the lesson. The visual supports provided through the **Student Response Guide** help make the lessons accessible to students with sensory or physical impairments. For example, for students with hearing impairment, the Student Response Guide can be used when the teacher directions are also signed. Students may sign their answers instead of pointing to the Student Response Guide, but the response pages may be used to help increase understanding. For students with visual impairments, it will be important that they are actively involved in the hands-on experiment so that the teacher directions have meaning. The vocabulary may be adapted to the students' current form of text access (e.g., Braille, raised pictures). Students with physical impairments who cannot point to the responses in the Student Response Guide may be able to respond using eyegaze or with assistive technology. For some students, the concepts taught in these lessons may be challenging, but it's important for all students to have the opportunity to learn. If students show difficulty mastering the vocabulary words and concept statements, select an alternative goal for lesson mastery. As an example, the student may point to or look at the object that shows the concept described (e.g., "Look at the chemical reaction").

Assistive and instructional technologies can promote students' participation in lessons aligned with general education curriculum (Erikson & Koppenhaver, 1997). The curriculum was piloted with students who are verbal and nonverbal, including those with physical, visual, and hearing impairments. Students may use their augmentative or alternative communication (AAC) systems or eyegaze systems to indicate their responses during the science lessons. The scripted lessons in Teaching to Standards: Science describe ways to meet the needs of students who use assistive technology, those who have visual impairments, and those who may not be making symbolic connections and need additional prompting. The Student Response Guide is provided as a pdf file on the CD-ROM in the event that additional modification of response mode is required. With students who require such support, it's important to create the adapted responses in preparation of the lesson. AAC devices should also be preprogrammed before beginning the lesson.

Safety rules

One of the most functional applications of these science lessons is the teaching of safety rules. Each lesson contains a reminder to review the safety rules found in the curriculum. It's important to display the **Safety Rules for Science Class** poster and to refer to it while reviewing the rules. Sometimes during the lesson there may be incidental learning opportunities to review the rules. For example, if something spills or breaks, review the rule about getting help from a teacher. An important message to students is to not eat science. Although some of the materials are edible, if eating is attempted, it's important to circumvent eating and say: "We do not eat science."

The KWHL chart

A Know/Want/How/Learn (KWHL) chart is included in Teaching to Standards: Science. The purpose of the KWHL chart is to help students work through the inquiry process and to serve as a reminder of how previous questions were answered. The final column (L for learned) serves as a review of what the students learned during the lesson. After steps 3, 4, 5, 6, and 12 of the inquiry lesson, record student answers as well as preferred answers in the corresponding areas of the KWHL chart. A blank KWHL chart for students is provided in Appendix B and can be printed from the CD-ROM. Throughout the lesson, record answers on the poster-size KWHL chart as a model for the class. Have students record their individual responses on the chart provided in Appendix B. Students also have the opportunity to record their personal predictions (step 6) of the outcome of the experiment on their personal KWHL charts. This record will serve as a reminder of student responses and can be reviewed at the end of the lesson.

ScienceWork and functional applications

Students with moderate-to-severe developmental disabilities are more likely to learn the science concepts if they have many opportunities for learning and using what they have learned. In addition to teaching the lessons across as many days as needed for learning to occur, students may benefit from extension activities. ScienceWork is one way to extend the activities. The ScienceWork stories and comprehension activities may be completed in class or sent home for additional practice. A pdf of ScienceWork is included on the CD-ROM so individual pages may be printed.

Students also need to see ways the concepts apply in their everyday lives. Whenever possible, find ways to use the science concepts in school and community contexts. Here are some examples:

1. **Earth unit:** A trip to a science museum may provide many examples of fossils and may offer displays of Earth's layers. Encourage students to recycle their snack containers. Also, a movie of a volcanic eruption or earthquake may be useful.

2. **Biology unit:** This unit provides the opportunity to review important health concepts. Students learn about "live" cells. This unit will also help them understand what causes sickness and how washing hands can help them stay healthy.

3. **Waters unit:** The daily weather report provides an opportunity to review precipitation. Changing weather can also provide naturally occurring examples of condensation (e.g., on the classroom windows on a cold day) or evaporation (e.g., a cup of cold water left outside on a hot day). This unit also provides the opportunity to encourage water conservation when washing hands, dishes, or other items.

4. **Chemistry unit:** Some knowledge of chemicals is important when handling cleaning supplies. For example, some floor cleaners require adding water to powder to make a solution. Some cause chemical reactions (e.g., jewelry cleaner). Students also need to know that some chemicals are harmful. The science rules can help teach not ingesting chemicals like cleaning supplies.

Documenting students' progress

Teaching to Standards: Science provides several ways to monitor students' progress. One way to monitor progress is to note those steps students have mastered and those that require more intensive support. The **Assessment and Planning Form** (see Appendix C) can be used

to track student progress throughout a unit of study. Opportunities for generalization to other settings or inclusive activities (e.g., working with a peer tutor to learn how to use a microscope) should also be noted on this form. However, if students do not have opportunities to attend an inclusive science class in a general education setting, the Assessment and Planning Form may be used to record opportunities to generalize concepts in the wider school or local community (e.g., help locate and label recyclable containers in the school, indicate the chance of precipitation each day on the classroom bulletin board).

The Assessment and Planning Form is also a plan to help students generalize concepts learned in the science unit to other settings. By dating the plan, you can revisit and update it to monitor student progress. This plan may be used in conjunction with Individualized Education Program (IEP) progress reports, noting progress on individual skills such as understanding the science concept presented. See a completed sample on page 14.

In our field test of these units, we also tested students on their knowledge of the core vocabulary by having them identify the sight words and the pictures, and then matching the words to the pictures. It may also be helpful to determine if the student can complete the concept statement for the unit. **The Progress Monitoring Form** (see Appendix D) may be useful for monitoring student progress in this way. A completed sample is provided on page 14.

A third way to monitor a student's progress is to review how the student responds to the steps in the inquiry-based lesson. In each lesson, a task analysis describes the step-by-step teaching procedure and the expected student response. Graph the number of independent correct responses, if desired.

Assessment and planning form

Student's name ___Lilli___   Date of planning ___3/28___

Core concept of the lesson ___Fossils are imprints that tell us about the past.___

	Evidence of learning	Changes needed in instruction to improve learning
Core skill Has the student mastered the core concept? Has the student mastered the vocabulary?	Lilli identifies the words model, layers, fossil, and recycle and matches them to pictures. She confuses core and crust because they both begin with "c." Lilli knows the core concept.	Lilli is keeping pace with the class. She is ahead in her vocabulary acquisition. She may need some help distinguishing the two words that begin with "c." Let's try highlighting the second letter and then fading this.
Functional applications Does the student apply the skill to real-life contexts?	When asked if the fossils are old or new, Lilli signed "old." She now points out other things in her environment as old and new.	A field trip to the museum is planned for the class to see fossils.
Conceptual generalization Does the student show understanding of the concept versus repeating a memorized response?	Although Lilli now understands fossils are old and what old is, she may not really understand what a fossil is.	Use the museum trip to build understanding. Introduce novel pictures to check for understanding.
Inclusion How has the student applied the skill during general education lessons?	Lilli will point to the picture of fossils in the textbook when her peer partner asks.	Lilli is building understanding of fossils through class activities like making a fossil imprint.
Next steps What is the next step for learning?	Lilli is ready to move to the next lesson with her class.	Begin providing support for Lilli to learn the next concept statement: "Plate movements cause changes to the Earth's crust."

Progress monitoring form

Student's name ___Lilli___   Semester ___Fall 2009___

Unit: ☒ Earth ☐ Biology ☐ Waters ☐ Chemistry   Lesson ___Lesson 2: Fossils___

Key: − error + independent correct M model/prompt

Dates	3/24	3/25	3/26	3/27	3/28
Picture cards					
model	M	M	+	+	+
core	M	M	M	M	M
crust	M	M	M	M	M
layers	M	M	+	+	+
fossil	M	M	+	+	+
recycle	M	M	+	+	+
Word cards					
model	M	M	+	+	+
core	M	M	+	M	M
crust	M	M	+	M	M
layers	M	M	+	−	+
fossil	M	M	+	−	+
recycle	M	M	+	−	+
Picture/word card match					
model	M	M	+	−	+
core	M	M	M	M	M
crust	M	M	M	M	+
layers	M	M	+	−	+
fossil	M	M	+	−	+
recycle	M	M	M	−	+
Concept statement: Fossils are imprints that tell us about the past.					
	M	M	+	−	+

Background

CONCEPTUAL FOUNDATION AND RESEARCH

Teaching to Standards: Science uses a structured, inquiry-based approach. The teacher provides hands-on problems to investigate and the procedures and materials for the investigation, but the students discover the relationships. For many students with moderate-to-severe disabilities, this may be their first experience with this type of learning.

Inquiry-based instruction is characterized by several components. Magnusson and Palincsar (1995) describe the components as:

- **Engagement**—In this component, the learning task is initiated. The engagement activity makes connections between past learning experiences and the present learning experience. It also anticipates the current activities and organizes students' thinking toward the learning outcomes of current activities.

- **Investigation**—This component may involve either first-hand investigations of physical phenomena or information gathering from secondary sources such as books or human experts. The investigation is planned, and specific attention is paid to what information or data need to be collected and how that will be achieved. It's important that the data students collect has patterns the students determine and describe.

- **Description of relationships**—This component consists of discussions about the investigation, and it focuses on the patterns observed by the students. Identification of patterns is a process requiring comparisons of objects or events that appear to be related and descriptions of the nature of the relationship. Students are guided toward topics or contexts that lead them to the "discovery."

- **Construct explanations**—This component is a formal explanation of the investigation. Students are guided to consider the presence of relevant scientific knowledge, and if so, what it means. At this point, if feasible, explanations should be tested.

- **Reporting of findings**—In this component, students use an array of response possibilities to represent their thinking (e.g., drawing, demonstration, print, oral description). The concepts learned can be reinforced using literal questioning.

RESEARCH ON INQUIRY-BASED SCIENCE LEARNING

Research on students without disabilities

Schneider and Renner (1980) investigated the use of inquiry instruction (i.e., the learning cycle) and formal instruction (the use of oral explanation sessions, motion pictures and filmstrips, textbooks, questions and problems, supervised study, and teacher demonstrations) on the acquisition of science concepts by ninth graders. The researchers found that the inquiry group outscored the formal instruction group on three-months-after-instruction examinations pertaining to the science concepts taught and concluded that use of inquiry instruction to teach science is justified for students at the concrete level.

Shymansky, Kyle, and Alport (1983) conducted a meta-analysis on 105 experimental studies dealing with the effects of new science curricula versus traditional science curricula on student performance. The researchers defined "new" science curricula as having the following characteristics: (a) was developed after 1955; (b) emphasized the nature, structure, and processes of science; (c) integrated laboratory activities as an integral part of the class routine; and (d) emphasized higher cognitive skills and appreciation of science. "Traditional" curricula (a) were developed or patterned after a program developed prior to 1955; (b) emphasized facts, laws, theories, and applications; and (c) used lab activities as verification exercises or as secondary applications of previously covered concepts. The researchers found that the new curricula had a positive impact on student performance criteria that included achievement, process skills, analytic skills, related skills (e.g., reading, math), and other areas (e.g., creativity, logical thinking).

Research on students who have mild disabilities

Research involving the use of inquiry-based instruction to teach science shows that this method can be successful with students who have or do not have disabilities. However, a gap often exists between research and practice in the classroom. To lessen the gap, Magnusson and Palincsar (1995) describe a planning and enactment heuristic to facilitate guided inquiry in the classroom. Guided inquiry is a blend of an inquiry-based approach (i.e., students are involved in direct exploration and manipulation of the physical world driven by questions about what and how to inquire) and a conceptual-change approach (i.e., opportunities are included for students to compare understandings they have previously constructed). Guided inquiry is also concerned with students having meaningful contexts in which to investigate. The heuristic proposed by Magnusson and Palincsar indicates to the teachers which types of activities the students must participate in to reach the goals of science education. The steps include asking a guiding question, engaging the students in the inquiry, investigating and describing relationships, constructing explanations, and reporting findings.

The research conducted on the use of inquiry-based science instruction for students with

mild disabilities confirms that the method is successful for this student population (Magnusson & Palincsar). Students with mild disabilities who were instructed with an inquiry-based method made more progress than students who were instructed using a direct instruction approach, a textbook approach, and a hands-on only approach. Scruggs and Mastropieri (1995) also found that students with intellectual disabilities may need "something more" than inquiry-based instruction alone. In the studies reviewed, the "something more" used to accommodate for intellectual deficits were adaptations such as reducing vocabulary demands, using graphic organizers, providing multiple presentations, asking carefully structured questions, familiarizing students with the science materials, and using guided coaching. The use of these accommodations illustrates that inquiry can be successfully adapted for students with intellectual deficits.

Research on students who have moderate-to-severe disabilities

Because the original framework of scientific inquiry is based on a developmental model of student learning, some may question its applicability to students with significant developmental disabilities who may not have achieved age expectations as described in Piagetian theory. Although models of intellectual development were once applied to this population, instruction based on mental age/stage is no longer considered appropriate (Browder, Spooner, Ahlgrim-Delzell, Flowers, Algozzine, & Karvonen, 2004; Browder, Trela, Courtade, Jimenez, & Knight, 2008). In contrast, this research is based on the premise that using inquiry-based instruction does not require a mental age assessment or achievement of a certain intellectual stage. Instead, teachers can accommodate for students' intellectual deficits using modifications and adaptations.

There is limited research on teaching science to students with moderate-to-severe disabilities. In a comprehensive review, Courtade, Spooner, and Browder (2007) identified 11 studies that taught science skills found in the National Science Education Standards to students who have significant cognitive disabilities. Although the science studies conducted with students who have significant disabilities produced successful results, the extent of the skills is limited. The instructional skills taught in 8 of the 11 studies fell under Content Standard F (Science in Personal and Social Perspectives) of the National Science Education Content Standards. Two studies conducted research that included describing relative position (Taber, Alberto, Hughes, & Seltzer, 2002; Taber, Alberto, Seltzer, & Hughes, 2003), which fell under Content Standard B (Physical Science). One study (Browder & Shear, 1996) conducted research about teaching weather-related sight words, which fell under Content Standard D (Earth and Space Science). Skills that fall under other content standards (i.e., Science as Inquiry, Life Science, Science and Technology, and History and Nature of Science) have not been addressed via research. Furthermore, because the students were not being taught process skills, their generalization of learning to other science skills may be limited.

However, the instructional procedures used in the studies are research-based. For example, the use of a task analysis to break skills down into segments was commonly used (Gast, Winterling, Wolery, & Farmer, 1992; Marchand-Martella, Martella, Christensen, Agran, & Young, 1992; Spooner, Stem, & Test, 1989; Watson, Bain, & Houghton, 1992; Winterling, Gast, Wolery, & Farmer, 1992). In general, these studies followed applied behavior analysis methodology of operationalizing behavior, using procedures to promote and transfer stimulus control from teacher prompting to stimulus materials, and the use of feedback and reinforcement of correct responses (Alberto & Troutman, 1999).

Courtade, Browder, Spooner, and DiBiase (2008) investigated the use of an inquiry-based approach with students who have moderate intellectual disabilities (see summary in Appendix A). Teachers increased their use of the components of an inquiry-based approach after receiving training on this method with specific guidance for steps to follow to plan science lessons. Students also increased their independent skills in participating in the inquiry-based lessons.

Teaching to Standards: Science builds on the research of Courtade, Browder, Spooner, and DiBiase, as well as the foundation of studies showing positive outcomes for students without disabilities or with mild disabilities. This curriculum was field tested with teachers in an urban school system with students who have both intellectual disabilities and autism. All lesson plans have been implemented by at least five different teachers. Although an evidence-based practice for teaching science to this population does not yet exist, this curriculum was developed using a thorough review of prior research. Every lesson plan was also carefully scrutinized by a content expert in science education for accuracy of scientific concepts and importance to core learning.

THE SCIENCE CONTENT STANDARDS

In addition to understanding inquiry and the research on teaching science, it's also important to be familiar with the science content standards as defined by the National Science Education Standards (NSES). Most state standards are organized with the same or similar standards. Teachers are encouraged to locate their state standards to see which of these standards are represented. The science content standards are as follows:

- Science as Inquiry
- Physical Science
- Life Science
- Earth and Space Science

- Science and Technology
- Science in Personal and Social Perspectives
- History and Nature of Science

STEPS FOR TEACHING TO A SCIENCE STANDARD

By collaborating with science educators, special educators can develop lessons that are conceptually sound and meaningful. The first step in developing lessons is to target an outcome for learning. The following steps can help with this process.

1. Identify one or more priority standards for the student's grade level. Begin by identifying the student's assigned grade level. Your state may have a document to help identify priority standards to be taught in science in that grade level. If not, ask a science teacher to help you identify key content or the "big idea" for a given area of science. For example, a sixth-grade standard and subgoals from Earth and Science is as follows:

Standard: The learner will build an understanding of the geological cycles, forces, processes, and agents which shape the lithosphere.

Subgoals:

- Evaluate the forces that shape the lithosphere including crustal plate movement, volcanic activity, earthquakes.
- Examine earthquake and volcano patterns.
- Evaluate the ways in which human activities have affected Earth's pedosphere and the measures taken to control the impact: vegetative landcover, agriculture, land use.

2. Consider the critical function or essence of the standard. Although the example standard seems ambitious for students with moderate-to-severe disabilities, it can be made more accessible if the key concept is clearly understood. To understand the example standard, we collaborated with a science curriculum expert to discuss both the concepts to be learned and how the standard is typically taught. We learned that the "critical function" of this standard (i.e., the essence) is to understand what natural and man-made events change the crust of the Earth.

3. Identify a student outcome. To target a student outcome, it's important to continue collaboration with a science educator so that the core concept of the standard is retained. One possible outcome for this standard is for the student to use pictures with word captions to indicate which forces cause certain changes in the Earth's crust. The student will also need to learn symbols for key concepts like precipitation and crust.

4. Make certain learning is meaningful. Students with moderate-to-severe disabilities need to apply new learning to their daily lives for it to be meaningful. One way to be certain the science learning is meaningful is to use picture symbols, photographs, and other media to show the concept. Students may also be asked to identify something in their surroundings that shows the concept (e.g., how water has affected the Earth's crust in their community). Science lessons are also an opportunity for students to extend their use of assistive technology. They may learn to access a website using switch activation or use new vocabulary on an alternative or augmentative communication (AAC) device. An inquiry-based approach provides students with opportunities for decision-making so they learn new self-determination skills, like identifying what they would like to learn and how they might find out about the concept. They may also evaluate the outcome of a learning experience. Science is also embedded in daily experiences. Becoming aware of the science in our daily lives can be part of making this content meaningful. For example, students may learn about how health is affected by the environment.

Unit  Earth

Lesson 1 Earth's layers

Concept

The Earth has different layers.

Background

In this lesson, students begin to learn about the Earth's composition. They learn that the Earth has layers. Since the use of models to represent a concept may be new to students, this lesson begins with a story about models. The story introduces a model of the Earth and explains why we use models in science.

Materials

- Model of Earth
- Rocks, gravel, sand
- Clear plastic cups, 1 per student and 1 for demonstration
- Picture and word cards for model, core, crust, layers, fossil, recycle
- Illustration of Earth's layers
- KWHL chart
- Safety Rules for Science Class poster
- Student Response Guide, pages 10–20
- ScienceWork, pages 8–11 and 82–84

BRING FROM HOME Post-it® notes (1" x 2"), zip-tight plastic sandwich bags

Preparation

Prepare one bag of rocks, gravel, and sand per student and one for yourself, by placing a small amount of each in zip-tight plastic sandwich bags. Cut Post-it® notes into thirds so each student has 3 and you have 3. Using the Post-it® notes, prepare labels that say Layer 1: core, Layer 2: mantle, and Layer 3: crust.

Vocabulary

Teach picture symbols and sight words for this unit (see pages 30–32) to familiarize students with the vocabulary introduced in this lesson.

Engage

STEP 1		
Materials	**Procedure**	**Follow-up**
<ul><li>Model of the Earth</li><li>Small bags of rocks, gravel, sand</li><li>Labels</li><li>Clear plastic cups</li><li>ScienceWork, pages 82–84: **Using models in science**</li></ul>	Engage the students by telling them: **Today in science we're going to learn about the Earth and what it is made of. Since the Earth is so big, we'll use a model of the Earth to learn about it. Let's read about models first.** Read **Using models in science** to students and have them follow along in their ScienceWork books. Show the model of the Earth and tell the students the model represents the Earth because the whole Earth is too big to hold and the layers are too hard to see. Point out the layers on the Earth's model.	
	Say: **Let's get started with our experiment.** Place the materials and the labels in front of the students. Invite students to examine the materials for a few moments, make comments, and ask questions.	If students ask, "What are these?" say: **Good question.**

 Engage

STEP 2

Materials	Procedure	Follow-up
• Model of the Earth • Small bags of rocks, gravel, sand • Picture and word cards for model • Student Response Guide, page 10: **What is this?**	Hold up each bag one at a time and ask: **What do you think is in this bag? Make a guess.** Give each student a chance to guess before giving feedback. Remember, you do want students to make guesses in an inquiry lesson. Have each student respond orally with "rocks," "sand," or "gravel"; use an AAC device to respond; or point to responses on the Student Response Guide page. Prompt students who don't have symbol use to look at the contents of the bags and to touch the pictures in the Student Response Guide. For example, say: **These are rocks. You're looking at rocks.**	Praise correct responses. If students give an incorrect answer, say: **That's a good guess.** Then give a brief reason why the choice isn't the best response. For example, for "marbles," say: **That's a good guess. It looks a bit like marbles, but it's actually gravel.** Explain to students: **The materials are all from the Earth. This is a model of the Earth. This is a picture of a model, and this word says model. Say "model."** Have them touch the model of Earth, and the picture and word cards for model.

STEP 3

Materials	Procedure	Follow-up
• Small bags of rocks, gravel, sand • KWHL chart • Student Response Guide, page 11: **What do you know?**	Point to the rocks and ask: **What do you know about a rock?** Have the students tell something they know about a rock. Have each student respond orally, use an AAC device to respond, or point to responses on the Student Response Guide page to say it's from the Earth, it's hard, and it's dug from the ground. Prompt students who don't have symbol use to look at the contents of the bag and to touch the picture of the rock in the Student Response Guide. For example, say: **You're looking at the rock. It's hard.** Repeat the question for the gravel and the sand.	Praise correct responses and say: **Yes, it's hard, it's dug from the ground, and it comes from the Earth.** Correct inappropriate answers by giving a brief reason why the response isn't the best response. For example, if "It runs fast" is chosen, say: **I don't think it runs fast. The rock isn't moving. But can you dig up rocks?** On the KWHL chart, record the correct answers in the "Know (K)" column. Draw a line to separate the responses for each: the rocks, the gravel, and the sand.

Engage

	STEP 4	
Materials	**Procedure**	**Follow-up**
• Small bags of rocks, gravel, sand • KWHL chart • Student Response Guide, page 12: **What do you want to know?**	Point to the materials and ask: **What do you want to know about the rocks, the gravel, and the sand?** Have students tell anything they might want to know about the materials. Have students respond orally, use their AAC devices to respond, or point to responses on the Student Response Guide page. Prompt students who don't have symbol use to choose any picture response. Provide feedback to students to help build meaning.	Acknowledge any response. For example, if "Will the materials bubble?" is chosen, say: **It would be interesting to find out if they will bubble.** Guide students to the answer: "What do the materials look like in the Earth?" **I would like to know what the materials look like in the Earth. How about you?** On the KWHL chart, record this response in the "Want (W)" column.

Investigate and describe relationships

	STEP 5	
Materials	**Procedure**	**Follow-up**
• KWHL chart • Student Response Guide, page 13: **How can we find out?**	While pointing to the "W" column on the KWHL chart, restate: **We want to know what the materials look like in the Earth.** Then ask: **How can we find out?** Have each student respond orally, use an AAC device to respond, point to a response on the Student Response Guide page, or pantomime making a model.	If students give alternate correct answers or incorrect answers, give a brief demo or explanation. For example, if they answer "Pour water on the rocks," pour water into the bag of rocks and say: **That didn't give us much information, What else can we do?** After several students respond, acknowledge the one who answers "Make a model of the Earth," or point to the preferred response and say: **I think the easiest way to find out is to make a model of the Earth.** On the KWHL chart, record responses in the "How (H)" column. Circle "Make a model of the Earth."

Investigate and describe relationships

STEP 6

Materials	Procedure	Follow-up
• Bags of rocks, gravel, sand • Labels • Clear plastic cups • KWHL chart • Safety Rules for Science Class poster • Student Response Guide, page 14: **What do you think will happen?**	Review the safety rules for science listed on the poster. Distribute one cup; one set of bags of rocks, gravel, and sand; and the labels to each student. Keep one set of materials to make your own model for the students to see. Say: **We'll each make a model of the Earth by pouring these materials into a clear cup. We'll pour the Earth materials from these bags** (point to the bags) **one at a time into our containers. Then we'll look at the materials and decide if they are mixed together or are in layers. Do you think the Earth's materials will be mixed or will be in layers?**	
	Have each student make a prediction by responding orally, using an AAC device to respond, pointing to a response on the Student Response Page, or nodding when you say "mixed" or "in layers."	Tally the students' answers—how many said the materials will be mixed and how many said they'll be in layers—and record them in the open area at the bottom of the KWHL chart to refer to at the end of the lesson.

Investigate and describe relationships

STEP 7

Materials	Procedure	Follow-up
• Bags of rocks, gravel, sand • Clear plastic cups • Labels	Say: **You each just made a prediction. Some of you said the materials will be mixed together, and some said the materials will be in layers. Let's find out.** First demonstrate constructing the model. Pour the sand into your plastic cup and add the label "Layer 1: core." Have the students do the same with their sand, plastic cups, and labels. Then pour the gravel into your cup and add the label "Layer 2: mantle." Have the students do the same with their models. Finally, pour the rocks into the cup and add the label "Layer 3: crust." Have the students do the same. Help the students count the layers of materials. Say: **This is layer 1** (point to the sand). **It's called the core. This is layer 2** (point to the gravel). **It's called the mantle. This is layer 3** (point to the rocks). **It's called the crust.** Count the layers together: **1, 2, 3 layers.**	Describe aloud what happens (e.g., **Here's another layer**), and encourage the students to tell what they see. Be sure students with visual impairments actively participate in the experiment (e.g., by pouring the materials or by feeling the materials before you put them in the cups).

Investigate and describe relationships

STEP 8

Materials	Procedure	Follow-up
• Clear cup with layers of sand, gravel, and rocks labeled • Student Response Guide, page 15: **What's the same?**	Hold up a cup and say: **Here are 3 layers of the Earth. The Earth has layers just like this. We call the layers the core, the mantle, and the crust. Here they are: the core, the mantle, and the crust of the Earth.** (Point to the sand, the gravel, and the rocks.) **How are they the same?** Have each student respond orally, use an AAC device to respond, or point to a response on the Student Response Guide page to say they're in layers and they're from the Earth. Prompt students who don't have symbol use to look at or touch the layers in the cup after another student correctly identifies that they're in layers and they're from the Earth.	Praise correct responses: **Yes, they're in layers, and they're from the Earth. That makes them the same.** If the students are not making a choice or are making an incorrect choice, say: **Touch the layer called the core. Touch the layer called the crust. Now touch the mantle. These materials have not mixed. They're still in layers. They are layers of Earth's materials. That makes them the same. They're in layers and they are from Earth.**

STEP 9

Materials	Procedure	Follow-up
• Clear cup with layers of sand, gravel, and rocks labeled • Student Response Guide, page 16: **What's different?**	Hold up a cup again and say: **Here are 3 layers of the Earth. Look at the first layer, the core** (point to the sand), **and the second layer, the mantle** (point to the gravel). **Now look at the third layer, the crust** (point to the rocks). **These are all layers. But how are they different?** Have each student respond orally, use an AAC device to respond, or point to a response on the Student Response Guide page to say they are different types of materials. Prompt students who don't have symbol use to look at (or touch) the layers on a cup.	Praise correct responses: **Yes, they're different types of materials. One layer is made of sand, one layer is made of gravel, and another layer is made of rocks. They're made of different materials.** If the students are not making a choice or are making an incorrect choice, hold up one cup and say: **What types of materials are the layers? Rocks, gravel, and sand are 3 types of materials. They are different types of materials.**

Construct explanation

STEP 10

Materials	Procedure	Follow-up
<ul><li>Clear cup with layers of sand, gravel, and rocks labeled</li><li>Picture and word cards for model, core, crust, layers</li><li>Student Response Guide, page 17: **What scientific discovery did we make?**</li></ul>	Read the scientific discovery statement once: **The Earth has different layers.** Say: **Let's review what we did. First we created a model of the Earth by adding the Earth's materials to our containers.** Put the picture and word cards for model in front of your cup.	
	Give students a turn to do the same (i.e., put the picture and word cards in front of their models). For students who don't respond, have them put the picture card with the materials and then guide them to match the word card. Other students may be prompted to look at the materials while you or a peer places the picture and word cards. Say: **We added sand to make Layer 1, the core.** Put the picture and word cards for core in front of your cup and say: **This is the picture for core, and this word says core. Say "core."**	Give praise: **Yes, this is a model of the Earth. Say "model."**
	Give students a turn to do the same (i.e., put the picture and word cards for core in front of their models). For students who don't respond, have them put the picture card with the materials and then guide them to match the word card. Other students may be prompted to look at the materials while you or a peer places the picture and word cards.	Give praise: **Yes, this layer is like the core of the Earth. Say "core."**

(Step continues)

Construct explanation

Materials	Procedure	Follow-up
	Say: **Next we added gravel to the container to make Layer 2, the mantle. Finally, we added rocks to make Layer 3, the Earth's crust.** Put the picture and word cards for crust in front of your cup. **This is the picture for crust, and this word says crust. Say "crust."**	
	Give students a turn to do the same (i.e., put the picture and word cards for crust in front of their models). For students who don't respond, have them put the picture card with the materials and then guide them to match the word card. Other students may be prompted to look at the materials while you or a peer places the picture and word cards. Touch each layer and count them: **1, 2, 3. The materials did not mix together. They're in layers.** Give each student a turn to count the layers. Put the picture and word cards for layers in front of your cup. Say: **This is the picture for layers, and this word says layers. Say "layers."**	Give praise: **Yes, this layer is like the crust of the Earth. Say "crust."**
	Give students a turn to do the same (i.e., put the picture and word cards for layers in front of their models). For students who don't respond, have them put the picture card with the materials and then guide them to match the word card. Other students may be prompted to look at the materials while you or a peer places the picture and word cards. Read the scientific discovery statement again, pointing to the words on the Student Response Guide page as you read and having the students follow along. Point to the layers on a cup.	Give praise: **Yes, these are like the layers of the Earth. Say "layers."**

Report

STEP 11		
Materials	**Procedure**	**Follow-up**
• Clear cup with layers of sand, gravel, and rocks labeled • KWHL chart • Student Response Guide, pages 18–19: **What did we find out?** and **Why?**	Say: **Let's review what we learned. I asked you if the Earth's materials would be mixed or be in layers.** Point to the predictions on the KWHL chart. **Some of you said mixed and some said in layers. Did the Earth's materials mix or stay in layers?** Have each student respond orally, use an AAC device to respond, point to a response on the Student Response Guide page, or nod yes or no.	Praise the students and then summarize: **Good, what happened is we made a model of the Earth by putting the Earth's materials in the container. The materials did not mix. They stayed in layers just like the layers of Earth do. We made a model that showed the core, the mantle, and the crust of the Earth. The Earth has materials that stay in layers.** If any students respond "mixed," point to the layers again. Write "The Earth has layers" in the open area at the bottom of the KWHL chart.
	Ask: **Why do the Earth's materials stay in layers?** Have each student respond orally, use an AAC device to respond, or point to a response on the Student Response Guide page to indicate that they stay in layers because they're different materials.	Point to a container and say: **Yes, the materials are different and so they stay in layers.** Scaffold for those who don't respond by saying: **Look at the sand. Now look at the gravel. Now look at the rocks. Are they the same or different?**

STEP 12		
Materials	**Procedure**	**Follow-up**
• KWHL chart • Student Response Guide, page 20: **What did we learn?** • Illustration of Earth's layers	Say: **Let's review what we learned. The Earth's materials do not mix. They stay in _____.** Have each student respond orally with "layers," use an AAC device to respond, or point to a response on the Student Response Guide page to fill in the blank. Show the illustration of the Earth's layers and review the layers.	Say: **Yes, the Earth's materials do not mix. They stay in layers.** Scaffold for students who say "a rainbow" by responding: **A rainbow does have many colors. The Earth has many materials. When the materials do not mix, we say they're in layers. The Earth has layers.** Point to and count layers in the cup. Write "The Earth has different layers" in the "Learned (L)" column of the KWHL chart.

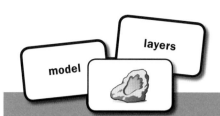

Teach vocabulary

Materials	Procedure	Follow-up
Picture cards: • model • core • crust • layers • fossil • recycle	Review the picture cards with students individually when possible. In this first round, give the student a prompt without delay (zero time delay). Place the picture cards in front of the student. Say: **Show me (model)** and point to the card as you ask the student to point (zero time delay). Shuffle the cards. Repeat this procedure for the remaining 5 cards.	If the student points correctly, give praise: **Good! You pointed to (model). Say (model).** If the student doesn't point, provide physical guidance to point.
	In this second round of vocabulary review, give the student up to 5 seconds to respond independently (5-second time delay). Shuffle the picture cards, place them in front of the student, and say: **Point to (model).** Repeat this process for the remaining 5 cards.	If the student points correctly, give praise: **Good! You pointed to (model) by yourself. Say (model).** If the student doesn't point, model pointing and say: **This is (model). Point to (model). Say (model).** If the student makes an error, point to the correct answer and say: **This is (model). Point to (model). Say (model).** Shuffle the cards and repeat this process for the remaining 5 cards.

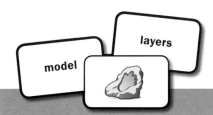

Teach vocabulary

Materials	Procedure	Follow-up
Word cards: • model • core • crust • layers • fossil • recycle	Review the word cards with students individually if possible. In this first round, give the student a prompt without delay (zero time delay). Place the word cards in front of the student. Say: **Show me (model)** and point to the card as you ask the student to point (zero time delay). Shuffle the cards. Repeat this procedure for the remaining 5 cards.	If the student points correctly, give praise: **Good! You pointed to (model). Say (model).** If the student doesn't point, provide physical guidance to point.
	In this second round of vocabulary review, give the student up to 5 seconds to respond independently (5-second time delay). Shuffle the word cards, place them in front of the student, and say: **Point to (model).** Repeat this process for the remaining 5 cards.	If the student points correctly, give praise: **Good! You pointed to (model) by yourself. Say (model).** If the student doesn't point, model pointing and say: **This is (model). Point to (model). Say (model).** If the student makes an error, point to the correct answer and say: **This is (model). Point to (model). Say (model).** Shuffle the cards and repeat this process for the remaining 5 cards.

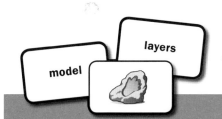

Teach vocabulary

Materials	Procedure	Follow-up
Picture and word cards: • model • core • crust • layers • fossil • recycle	In the first round, place the word cards in front of the student. Then hand a picture card to the student and say: **Match this picture to the word.** Match the picture card to the word card as you ask the student to match them (zero time delay). Shuffle the cards. Repeat this procedure for the remaining 5 cards.	If the student matches correctly, give praise: **Good! You matched the picture to the word. Say (model).** If the student doesn't match the cards, provide physical guidance to point.
	In a second round, give the student up to 5 seconds to match 2 cards independently (5-second time delay). Repeat this process for the remaining 5 cards.	If the student matches correctly, give praise: **Good! You matched the 2 cards by yourself. Say (model).** If the student doesn't match the cards, model matching and say: **This is (model). Match this card to the word (model). Say (model).** If the student makes an error, point to the correct answer and say: **This is (model). Match this card to (model). Say (model).** Shuffle the cards and repeat this process for the remaining 5 cards.

Reviewing vocabulary in a group

If reviewing vocabulary in a group, follow the format described, but have one student respond while you cue the others to watch. Pick a second student at random to repeat the response from time to time to be sure everyone is watching.

Extend and review lesson

Read the story on pages 8–9 in **ScienceWork** with the students. Help them apply the scientific concept they learned in this lesson to the story. Complete the exercise following the story together or send it home as homework.

Lesson 2 Fossils

Concept

Fossils are imprints that tell us about the past.

Background

In this lesson, students begin to learn about how we use Earth's materials. They learn about imprints and fossils and what they offer us (i.e., information about the past). The use of models to understand a concept may be new to students. Introduce the dinosaur as a model and explain why we use models in science.

Materials

- Dinosaur model
- Human model
- One silk leaf
- Modeling compound
- Picture and word cards for model, core, crust, layers, fossil, recycle
- KWHL chart
- Safety Rules for Science Class poster
- Student Response Guide, pages 21–31
- ScienceWork, pages 12–15 and 82–84

TO REPLENISH MATERIALS

Replenish the modeling compound with Model Magic® by Crayola or a similar product.

Preparation

Prepare for the lesson by making a model of a dinosaur fossil. Shape the modeling compound into a rock-like form. Press the dinosaur's foot into the "rock" and allow it to harden overnight.

Just before beginning the lesson, shape more modeling clay into rock-like forms; prepare 3 per student and 1 for demonstration.

Vocabulary

Review picture and sight word cards for this unit (see pages 30–32).

 **Engage**

STEP 1

Materials	Procedure	Follow-up
• Model of dinosaur fossil • ScienceWork, pages 82–84: **Using models in science**	Engage the students by telling them: **Today in science we're going to learn about fossils. Fossils were made by living things of long ago. We'll use a model of a fossil to learn about fossils. Let's read about models first.** Read **Using models in science** to students and have them follow along in their ScienceWork books.	
	Show the model of the dinosaur fossil and tell students: **This model represents a rock with a fossil in it that was made many years ago. Fossils like this one are hard to find, so we'll use this model to show what the fossil might be like.**	If students ask, "What is it?" say: **Good question.**

STEP 2

Materials	Procedure	Follow-up
• Model of dinosaur fossil • Picture and word cards for model • Student Response Guide, page 21: **What is this?**	Hold up the model of the dinosaur fossil and ask: **What do you think this is? Make a guess.** Give each student a chance to guess before giving feedback. Remember, you do want students to make guesses in an inquiry lesson. Have each student respond orally with "a fossil" or "a rock," use an AAC device to respond, or point to responses on the Student Response Guide page. Prompt students who don't have symbol use to look at the fossil with the footprint and say: **You're looking at a rock with a footprint in it. It's a fossil.**	Praise correct responses. If students give an incorrect answer, say: **That's a good guess.** Then give a brief reason why the choice isn't the best response. For example, for "a jellybean," say: **That's a good guess. It looks a bit like a jellybean, but it's actually a fossil.** After the students have guessed, guide them to point to the fossil. Explain to students that there is a footprint in the rock. Say: **A footprint is a kind of imprint. Imprints are marks made by pressure. For example, when an animal steps on wet clay, it makes an imprint of its foot on the clay. An imprint of a living thing from a long time ago is called a fossil. Here's the picture for model, and this word says model. Say "model."** Have them touch the model of the fossil, and the picture and word cards for model.

 **Engage**

STEP 3

Materials	Procedure	Follow-up
• Model of dinosaur fossil • KWHL chart • Student Response Guide, page 22: **What do you know?**	Point to the model of the dinosaur fossil and ask: **What do you know about this rock with the fossil in it?** Have the students tell something they know about the dinosaur fossil. Have each student respond orally, use an AAC device to respond, or point to responses on the Student Response Guide page to say it's old, it's hard, or it's an imprint. Prompt students who don't have symbol use to look at the fossil and to touch the picture of the imprint in the Student Response Guide. For example, say: **You're looking at a rock with a fossil in it. It's old.**	Praise correct responses. Correct inappropriate answers by giving a brief reason why the response isn't the best response. For example, if "It's soft" is chosen, say: **I don't think it's soft. Feel this. It's hard.** On the KWHL chart, record the correct answers in the "Know (K)" column.

STEP 4

Materials	Procedure	Follow-up
• Model of dinosaur fossil • KWHL chart • Student Response Guide, page 23: **What do you want to know?**	Point to the dinosaur fossil and ask: **What do you want to know about this rock with the fossil in it?** Have students tell anything they might want to know about the fossil. Have students respond orally, use their AAC devices to respond, or point to responses on the Student Response Guide page. Prompt students who don't have symbol use to choose any picture response.	Acknowledge any response. For example, if "What do rocks say?" is chosen, say: **I'm listening and I don't hear anything.** Guide students to the answer: "How do rocks get imprints in them?" Say: **I would like to know what made the imprint. How about you?** On the KWHL chart, record this response in the "Want (W)" column.

Investigate and describe relationships

STEP 5

Materials	Procedure	Follow-up
• Model of dinosaur fossil • KWHL chart • Student Response Guide, page 24: **How can we find out?**	While pointing to the "W" column on the KWHL chart, restate: We want to know what made the imprint on the rock. Then ask: How can we find out? Have each student respond orally, use an AAC device to respond, point to a response on the Student Response Guide page, or pantomime pressing an object into a rock to make an imprint.	If students give alternate correct answers or incorrect answers, give a brief demo or explanation. For example, if they answer "Use a microscope to find a dinosaur," say: I don't think we can find a dinosaur. What else could we do? After several students respond, acknowledge the one who answers "Make a fossil using a model" or point to the preferred response and say: I think the easiest way to find out is to make a fossil using a model. On the KWHL chart, record responses in the "How (H)" column. Circle "Make a fossil using a model."

STEP 6

Materials	Procedure	Follow-up
• Model of dinosaur fossil • Dinosaur and human models • Silk leaf • 3 rock-like forms • Safety Rules for Science Class poster • Student Response Guide, page 25: **What do you think will happen**	Review the safety rules for science class listed on the poster. Distribute the 3 rock-like forms to each student. Say: We'll press the model dinosaur, the model human, and the leaf into the clay rocks (point to the rock-like forms and models). We want to find out what made this fossil (point to the model of the dinosaur fossil). We'll make imprints of the dinosaur, the human, and the leaf in these rocks and compare them. What do you think will happen? What do you think made this imprint—a dinosaur, a leaf, or a human?	
	Have each student make a prediction by responding orally, using an AAC device to respond, pointing to a response on the Student Response Guide page, or nodding as you name the options.	Tally the students' answers—how many said a dinosaur, a leaf, or a human—and record them in the open area at the bottom of the KWHL chart to refer to at the end of the lesson.

Investigate and describe relationships

Materials	Procedure	Follow-up
• Model of dinosaur fossil • Dinosaur and human models • Silk leaf • 3 rock-like forms	Say: **You each just made a prediction. Some of you said the dinosaur made the imprint, some said the human, and some said the leaf. Let's find out.** Demonstrate pressing a dinosaur foot into the clay rock. Pass the dinosaur to the students so they each can do the same with their rocks. Press the human foot into the clay rock and pass it to the students to do the same. Repeat for the leaf. Say: **Look at the imprints you've made. Now let's compare the imprints to this fossil** (point to the model of the dinosaur fossil).	Describe aloud what happens, and encourage the students to tell what they see (e.g., "I see a footprint"). Be sure students with visual impairments actively participate in the experiment (e.g., by pressing the models into the clay rocks and by feeling the imprint after it's made).

Materials	Procedure	Follow-up
• 3 clay rocks (with imprints) • Student Response Guide, page 26: **What's the same?**	Hold up the 3 rocks with the new imprints and say: **Here are the 3 rocks from our experiment. What's the same about these rocks?** Have each student respond orally, use an AAC device to respond, or point to a response on the Student Response Guide page to say they are all fossils and they all have imprints. Prompt students who don't have symbol use to look at or touch the rocks after another student correctly identifies that the materials are fossils.	Praise correct responses: **Yes, they all are fossils. They all have imprints in them. That makes them the same.** If the students are not making a choice or are making an incorrect choice, hold up one rock at a time and say: **Touch all the fossils. Remember, we pressed a model dinosaur into this rock.** (Pretend to walk the dinosaur on the rock again.) **Then we pressed the foot of a human on this rock.** (Pretend to walk the person on the rock again.) **Finally, we pressed the leaf into this rock.** (Pretend to press the leaf on the rock again.) **They all have imprints. That makes them the same.**

Investigate and describe relationships

STEP 9

Materials	Procedure	Follow-up
• 3 clay rocks (with imprints) • Student Response Guide, page 27: **What's different?**	Hold up the clay rocks one at a time and say: **Look again at the fossils. Remember, we pressed the dinosaur foot into one rock. Then we pressed the human foot in the next rock. Finally, we pressed the leaf into the last rock. Now look at the rocks. What's different about them?** Have each student respond orally, use an AAC device to respond, or point to a response on the Student Response Guide page to say there are different imprints on the rocks. Prompt students who don't have symbol use to look at or touch one of the fossils and then touch the model that made the imprint.	Praise correct responses: **Yes, they have different imprints. The imprints are made from different things. This rock has an imprint from a dinosaur model** (point to the rock with the dinosaur footprint), **and this rock has an imprint from a human model** (point to the rock with the human footprint). **This rock has an imprint of a leaf** (point to the rock with the leaf imprint). If the students are not making a choice or are making an incorrect choice, hold up one rock at a time and say: **What do you see in this rock? We walked a dinosaur on the rock. The dinosaur foot left an imprint in the soft clay. That imprint is different than the leaf imprint.**

Construct explanation

STEP 10

Materials	Procedure	Follow-up
• 3 clay rocks (with imprints) • Picture and word cards for fossil • Student Response Guide, page 28: **What scientific discovery did we make?**	Read the scientific discovery statement once: **Fossils are imprints that tell us about the past.** Say: **Let's review what we did. First we pressed the model dinosaur on the soft clay rock** (touch the rock), **and we saw an imprint that told us a dinosaur walked on it. Then we pressed a human foot on the soft clay rock** (touch the rock), **and we saw an imprint that told us a person walked on it. Finally, we pressed a leaf on a soft clay rock** (touch the rock), **and we saw an imprint that told us a leaf fell on the rock. Imprints become fossils over time. Fossils are imprints that give scientists clues about where living things** (point to the dinosaur, the human, and the leaf) **came from.** Put the picture and word cards for fossil in front of the rocks and say: **This is the picture for fossil, and this word says fossil. Say "fossil."**	
	Give students a turn to do the same (i.e., put the picture and word cards in front of their rocks). For students who don't respond, have them put the picture cards with the materials and then guide them to match the word card. Other students may be prompted to look at the rocks while you or a peer places the picture and word cards. Read the scientific discovery statement again, pointing to the words on the Student Response Guide page as you read and having the students follow along.	Give praise: **Yes, this is a fossil. Fossils are imprints that tell us about the past. What happened is that the clay rock was soft when the dinosaur made a footprint in it. The footprint is an imprint. Now the clay is a model of a fossil. Remember, sometimes in science we need to use a model to help us learn about things we can't see or touch. A fossil is very old.**

Report

STEP 11

Materials	Procedure	Follow-up
• Model of dinosaur fossil • KWHL chart • Student Response Guide, pages 29–30: **What did we find out?** and **Why?**	Say: **Let's review what we found out. I asked you what you thought made this imprint** (point to the model of the dinosaur fossil). Point to the predictions on the KWHL chart. **Some of you said a dinosaur made it, some of you said a human made it, and others thought that a leaf made the imprint. In our experiment we made new imprints. So what do you think made this imprint?**	Praise the students and then summarize: **Good, the fossil was a dinosaur footprint. When we pressed the dinosaur, the human, and the leaf into the clay, only one imprint matched the fossil. The imprint matched the dinosaur's footprint. The imprint told us that a dinosaur had walked on that rock.** If any students respond "a leaf" or "a human," show the original fossil next to the new imprints and ask them to point to the one that looks the same. Write "A dinosaur made the imprint" in the open area at the bottom of the KWHL chart.
	Point to the model of the dinosaur fossil and ask: **Why can a rock tell us about the past?** Have each student respond orally, use an AAC device to respond, or point to a response on the Student Response Guide page to indicate that it has an imprint.	Point to the rock as you say: **Yes, the rock has an imprint that tells us about the past.** Scaffold for those who don't respond by asking: **When you look at the rock, how do you know the dinosaur walked on it?**

Report

STEP 12

Materials	Procedure	Follow-up
• KWHL chart • Student Response Guide, page 31: **What did we learn?**	Say: **Let's review what we learned. What do we call an imprint that tells us about the past?** Have each student respond orally with "a fossil," use an AAC device to respond, or point to a response on the Student Response Guide page.	Say: **Yes, we call an imprint about the past a fossil.** Scaffold for students who say "diamond" by rephrasing: **It's a rock, but does it have an imprint?** Write "Fossils are imprints that tell us about the past" in the "Learned (L)" column of the KWHL chart.

Review vocabulary

Materials: Picture and word cards for model, core, crust, layers, fossil, recycle

Procedure: Use the time-delay procedure to review each of the vocabulary words for the unit. See page 8 for the procedure.

Extend and review lesson

Read the story on pages 12–13 in **ScienceWork** with the students. Help them apply the scientific concept they learned in this lesson to the story. Complete the exercise following the story together or send it home as homework.

Lesson 3 Plate tectonics

Concept

Plate movements cause changes to the Earth's crust.

Background

In this lesson, students learn about tectonic plates and the way the Earth's crust is affected by plate movements. You'll be creating models of oceanic plates and continental plates (using graham crackers) to demonstrate two types of tectonic plate movement: (1) convergent plate movement—where two continental plates collide, forming mountains; and (2) transform plate movement—where two continental plates slide past each other, forming a faultline. Earthquakes occur when continental plates slide past each other. The graham cracker represents the continental crust. These are edible materials, but treat them as you would dangerous chemicals to teach students to be cautious with science materials.

Materials

- Clear plastic cup
- Photo of a mountain range
- Picture and word cards for model, core, crust, layers, fossil, recycle
- Illustration of the aftermath of an earthquake
- KWHL chart
- Safety Rules for Science Class poster
- Student Response Guide, pages 32–42
- ScienceWork, pages 16–18

BRING FROM HOME 4 graham crackers, wax paper, water

Preparation

Make the plate models (model 1 and model 2) ahead of time. Cut 2 sheets of wax paper so they are approximately 12" x 12". Place the wax paper on your working surface to protect it. Place 2 graham crackers onto each piece of wax paper side by side so the longest sides are aligned for each model you're creating. Fill the cup with water.

Vocabulary

Review picture and sight word cards for this unit (see pages 30–32).

Engage

STEP 1		
Materials	**Procedure**	**Follow-up**
• Model 1 • Model 2 • Illustration of the aftermath of an earthquake • Photo of a mountain range	Engage the students by showing them the pictures and telling them: **Today we'll use these materials** (point to the models) **to learn more about these pictures** (point to the pictures of the earthquake and mountains).	If students ask, "What are these?" say: **Good question.**

STEP 2		
Materials	**Procedure**	**Follow-up**
• Model 1 • Model 2 • Student Response Guide, page 32: **What is this?**	Point to the models one at a time and ask: **What do you think these are? Make a guess.** Give each student a chance to guess before giving feedback. Remember, you do want students to make guesses in an inquiry lesson. Have each student respond orally with "models," use an AAC device to respond, or point to responses on the Student Response Guide page. Prompt students who don't have symbol use to look at the materials and then guide them to touch the picture. For example, say: **You're looking at a model of Earth's crust. This is a model of the Earth's crust.** Show students the 2 models and say: **Today we'll use these models to learn more about the Earth's crust. Scientists have found that the Earth has layers. The top layer is the crust, and the crust has different plates. These are models of the Earth's crust and its plates.**	Praise correct responses. If students give an incorrect answer, say: **That's a good guess.** Then give a brief reason why the choice isn't the best response. For example, for "dogs," say: **I don't see any dogs. Dogs don't look like these models.**

Engage

STEP 3		
Materials	**Procedure**	**Follow-up**
• Model 1 • Model 2 • KWHL chart • Student Response Guide, page 33: **What do you know?**	Point to the materials representing the plates and say: **What do you know about these models?** Have the students tell something they know about the models. Have each student respond orally, use an AAC device to respond, or point to responses on the Student Response Guide page. Prompt students who don't have symbol use to look at each model and to touch the picture of the model in the Student Response Guide. For example, say: **You're looking at plates.**	Praise correct responses. Correct inappropriate answers by giving a brief reason why the response isn't the best response. For example, if "Plates are fast" is chosen, say: **Look at the models; they aren't moving fast** (point to the plates). **The models show plates found on the crust of Earth. Pretend this is the crust and these are plates.** On the KWHL chart, record the correct answers in the "Know (K)" column.

STEP 4		
Materials	**Procedure**	**Follow-up**
• Model 1 • Model 2 • KWHL chart • Student Response Guide, page 34: **What do you want to know?**	Point to the models and ask: **What do you want to know about these models?** Have students tell anything they might want to know about the models. Have students respond orally, use their AAC devices to respond, or point to responses on the Student Response Guide page. Prompt students who don't have symbol use to choose any picture response. Provide feedback to students to help build meaning.	Acknowledge any response. For example, if "What do the plates sound like?" is chosen, say: **It would be interesting to find out what they sound like.** Guide students to the answer: "What will happen if the plates move?" Say: **I would like to know what will happen if the plates move. How about you?** On the KWHL chart, record this response in the "Want (W)" column.

Investigate and describe relationships

STEP 5

Materials	Procedure	Follow-up
• Model 1 • Model 2 • KWHL chart • Student Response Guide, page 35: **How can we find out?**	While pointing to the "W" column on the KWHL chart, restate: We want to know what will happen if the plates move. Then ask: How can we find out? Have each student respond orally, use an AAC device to respond, point to a response on the Student Response Guide page, or pantomime a moving action.	If students give alternate correct answers or incorrect answers, give a brief demo or explanation. For example, if they answer "Watch the plates," let them look at the plates and say: That didn't give us much information. What else could we do? After several students respond, acknowledge the one who answers, "Move them," or point to the preferred response and say: I think the easiest way to find out is to move them. On the KWHL chart, record responses in the "How (H)" column. Circle "Move them."

STEP 6

Materials	Procedure	Follow-up
• Safety Rules for Science Class poster • Student Response Guide, page 36: **What do you think will happen?**	Review the safety rules for science listed on the poster. Say: The top layers of the Earth form these plates. We'll use our models to show how the plates move. First we'll move the plates in one model so the edges of the plates or the crust of the Earth bump into each other. Next we'll move the plates in the second model so the edges of the crust slide past each other. Then we'll look at the Earth's crust (point to the top of model as the Earth's crust) to see if it changed. Do you think the crust will change when the plates are moved—yes or no?	
	Have each student make a prediction by responding orally, using an AAC device to respond, pointing to a response on the Student Response Guide Page, or nodding.	Tally the students' answers—how many said yes and how many said no—and record them in the open area at the bottom of the KWHL chart to refer to at the end of the lesson.

Investigate and describe relationships

STEP 7

Materials	Procedure	Follow-up
<ul><li>Cup of water</li><li>Model 1</li><li>Model 2</li><li>Photo of a mountain range</li><li>Illustration of the aftermath of an earthquake</li></ul>	Say: **You just made a prediction. Some of you said yes, the Earth's crust will change when we move the plates. Some of you said no, the Earth's crust will not change when we move the plates. Let's find out.** Begin the first demonstration with model 1. Briefly dip the edge of the graham crackers in water and lay the wet sides together. Gently push the edges of the graham crackers into each other. The edges should bunch together and form a "mountain ridge" where the 2 crackers come together. Place the photo of the mountain range next to the model. Conduct the second demonstration with model 2. Gently slide the graham cracker pieces past each other. Small pieces might break off, and the edges will no longer be lined up evenly. This model illustrates a fault line. Place the illustration of the earthquake aftermath next to model 2.	Describe aloud what happens (e.g., **The plates are bunching up and forming a ridge; the plates are breaking apart and leaving some pieces behind**). Encourage the students to tell what they see. Be sure students with visual impairments actively participate in the experiment (e.g., by feeling the "mountain ridges" as the plates raise up and feeling the pieces that may have broken away from the plates).

Investigate and describe relationships

STEP 8

Materials	Procedure	Follow-up
• The changed model 1 • The changed model 2 • Student Response Guide, page 37: **What's the same?**	Point to the models and say: **Here are the models we used in our experiment. What's the same about these models?** Have each student respond orally, use an AAC device to respond, or point to a response on the Student Response Guide page to say the plates moved for both. Prompt students who don't have symbol use to look at or touch the models after another student correctly identifies that the plates moved for both.	Praise correct responses: **Yes, the plates moved in both models. That makes them the same.** If the students are not making a choice or are making an incorrect choice, say: **We had layers in each model. We call the layers plates. Each model has plates that moved. That makes them the same.**

STEP 9

Materials	Procedure	Follow-up
• The changed model 1 • The changed model 2 • Student Response Guide, page 38: **What's different?**	Point to the models and say: **Here are the models we used in our experiment. Look at each model. How are they different?** Have each student respond orally, use an AAC device to respond, or point to a response on the Student Response Guide page to say one has broken pieces and one has edges raised up. Prompt students who don't have symbol use to look at or touch the models after another student correctly identifies that one has broken pieces and one has edges raised up.	Praise correct responses: **Yes, the plates raised up in one model and broke into some pieces in the other. That makes them different.** If the students are not making a choice or are making an incorrect choice, point to the models and say: **Look at these models. The crust looks different after the plates were moved. In this one** (point to Model 1 showing the mountain formation), **the crust was pushed up when the 2 plates bumped into each other. In this one** (point to model 2 where the plates were slid past each other), **some pieces of the crust broke off and the plates are not even with each other anymore. The plates each moved in a different way. Each movement made the crust layer look different.**

Construct explanation

STEP 10

Materials	Procedure	Follow-up
<ul><li>Picture and word cards for crust</li><li>Photo of a mountain range</li><li>Illustration of the aftermath of an earthquake</li><li>Student Response Guide, page 39: **What scientific discovery did we make?**</li></ul>	Read the scientific discovery statement once: **Plate movement causes changes in the Earth's crust.** Say: **Let's review what we did. When the plates moved, they bumped into each other** (point to model 1). **Now there is this line, this ridge, that rose up between the 2 plates. When that happens to the Earth's crust, it forms a mountain range** (point to the photo of the mountain range). **Next, when we moved the plates on this model** (point to model 2), **the edges of the plates scraped against each other. It wasn't very smooth when the plates moved, so pieces of the plates got stuck and some pieces of the plates fell away from it. When that happens, you can feel an earthquake from the vibrations** (point to the illustration of the aftermath of an earthquake). Touch the top layer of each model as you put the picture and word card for crust in front of the models and say: **This is the picture for crust, and this word says crust. Say "crust."**	
	Give students a turn to do the same (i.e., put the picture and word card for crust in front of the models).	Give praise: **Yes, this is the crust. Plate movements cause changes in the Earth's crust.**

(Step continues)

Construct explanation

Materials	Procedure	Follow-up
	For students who don't respond, have them look at the top layer of the models as the explanation is given and then guide them to touch the crust layer on the models. Read the scientific discovery statement again, pointing to the words on the Student Response Guide page as you read and having the students follow along. Point to the models as you read.	

Report

STEP 11		
Materials	**Procedure**	**Follow-up**
• KWHL chart • Student Response Guide, pages 40–41: **What did we find out?** and **Why?**	Say: **Let's review what we learned. I asked you if moving the plates would change the Earth's crust.** Point to the predictions on the KWHL chart. **Some of you said yes and some no. Did the crust change when the Earth's plates moved?**	Praise the students and then summarize: **Yes, we saw the Earth's crust change when the plates moved. What happened is that the plates in our models moved in 2 different ways. This caused changes to the Earth's crust, or the top layer in our model.** If any students respond no, point to the models again and say: **Let's take a look at the models. This model has edges that are pushed up. This model has edges with parts broken off of it. The Earth's crust changed when the plates moved.** Write "Yes, crust changed" in the open area at the bottom of the KWHL Chart.
	Ask: **Why did the Earth's crust change?** Have each student respond orally, use an AAC device to respond, or point to a response on the Student Response Guide page to indicate that the crust changed because the plates moved.	Point to a model and say: **That's right, the Earth's crust changed because the plates moved.** Scaffold for those who don't respond by saying: **Remember, the crust was flat before the plates moved. Now, the crust on each model is different.**

Report

STEP 12		
Materials	**Procedure**	**Follow-up**
• KWHL chart • Student Response Guide, page 42 **What did we learn?**	Say: **Let's review what we learned. Changes to the Earth's crust are caused by _____.** Have each student respond orally with "plate movement," use an AAC device to respond, or point to a response on the Student Response Guide page to fill in the blank.	Say: **Yes, when plates move, they cause changes to the Earth's crust.** Scaffold for students who say "magic" by responding: **Sometimes the change can be so big that it seems like magic. It's the plate movement, which we can't always see, that causes a change to the Earth's crust.** Write "Changes to the Earth's crust are caused by plate movement" in the "Learned (L)" column of the KWHL chart.

Review vocabulary

Materials: Picture and word cards for model, core, crust, layers, fossil, recycle

Procedure: Use the time-delay procedure to review each of the vocabulary words for the unit. See page 8 for the procedure.

Extend and review lesson

Read the story on page 16 in **ScienceWork** with the students. Help them apply the scientific concept they learned in this lesson to the story. Complete the exercise following the story together or send it home as homework.

Lesson 4 Age of fossils

Concept

Earth's layers tell us the age of a fossil.

Background

In this lesson, students learn how the Earth's layers give clues about when a fossil was formed. The layers help us know which fossils are older, newer, or the same age as other fossils.

Materials

- Fossils (2 of each): bone, fish, arrowhead
- Clay in 3 different colors (brown, gray, white) to represent the Earth's layers
- Metal spoon
- Picture and word cards for model, core, crust, layers, fossil, recycle
- KWHL chart
- Safety Rules for Science Class poster
- Student Response Guide, pages 43–53
- ScienceWork, pages 19–21 and 85

 BRING FROM HOME 3" x 5" index card

Vocabulary

Review picture and sight word cards for this unit (see pages 30–32).

Preparation

- Three days before the lesson is scheduled, begin to make a model of the Earth's layers with the students observing. Using one color (brown) of clay—layer 1—press the bone into the clay. Write the date the bone was buried in layer 1 on the index card (e.g., 10/23). Stand the index card next to the clay, with the arrow pointing to the first day's layer.

- On the next day, with the students observing, roll out a second color (gray) of clay—layer 2—and press the arrowhead and fish into the second layer. Place the second layer on top of the first layer. On the same index card, label the date on which you buried the arrowhead and fish into layer 2. Return the index card next to the layers of clay, with arrows now pointing to the first and second layers.

- On day three, with the students observing, roll out the third color (white) of clay. Place the clay on top of layers 1 and 2 without any fossil being buried in it. On the same index card, label the date on which layer 3 was placed on the other 2 layers. Return the index card next to the layers of clay, with arrows now pointing to the first, second, and third layers. Then begin the experiment.

 **Engage**

STEP 1

Materials	Procedure	Follow-up
Model of Earth's layers	Engage the students by telling them: **Today we'll learn how scientists study the age of things like this.**	
	Place the model of Earth's layers in front of the students. Invite students to examine the model for a few moments, make comments, and ask questions.	If students ask, "What are these?" say: **Good question.**

STEP 2

Materials	Procedure	Follow-up
• Fossils: bone, fish, arrowhead • Model of Earth's layers • Student Response Guide, page 43: **What is this?**	Hold up each fossil one at a time and ask: **What do you think this is?** Give each student a chance to guess before giving feedback. Remember, you do want students to make guesses in an inquiry lesson. Have each student respond orally with "an arrowhead," "a fish," "a fossil," or "a bone"; use an AAC device to respond; or point to responses on the Student Response Guide page. Prompt students who don't have symbol use to look at each fossil and to touch the pictures in the Student Response Guide. For example, say: **This is an arrowhead. This is an arrow that someone used long ago.** After the students have guessed, guide them to point to the arrowhead, the fish, the fossil, and the bone. Say: **This arrowhead, fish, and bone are all fossils. They're very old.** Then point to the model of Earth's layers and say: **This is a model of Earth's layers. These are fossils** (point to the fossils), **or things that scientists find in the Earth.**	Praise correct responses. If students give an incorrect answer, say: **That's a good guess.** Then give a brief reason why the choice isn't the best response. For example, for "a stick," say: **That's a good guess. It looks like a stick, but it's a bone. You're looking at a bone.**

 Engage

STEP 3		
Materials	**Procedure**	**Follow-up**
• Fossils: bone, fish, arrowhead • KWHL chart • Student Response Guide, page 44: **What do you know?**	Point to the fossils and ask: **What do you know about these fossils?** Have the students tell something they know about the fossils. Have each student respond orally, use an AAC device to respond, or point to responses on the Student Response Guide page to say they're old, they feel hard, and they're found in the ground. Prompt students who don't have symbol use to look at the arrowhead and to touch the picture in the Student Response Guide. For example, say: **You're looking at an arrowhead. It's old.**	Praise correct responses and say: **Yes, this arrowhead is old and hard and found in the ground.** Correct inappropriate answers by giving a brief reason why the response isn't the best response. For example, if "They're loud" is chosen, say: **The objects aren't loud. I don't hear them at all. What else do we know about them?** On the KWHL chart, record the correct answers in the "Know (K)" column.

STEP 4		
Materials	**Procedure**	**Follow-up**
• Fossils: bone, fish, arrowhead • KWHL chart • Student Response Guide, page 45: **What do you want to know?**	Point to the fossils and ask: **What do you want to know about the fossils and the model of the layers of the Earth?** Have students tell anything they might want to know about the fossils. Have students respond orally, use their AAC devices to respond, or point to responses on the Student Response Guide page. Prompt students who don't have symbol use to choose any picture response. Provide feedback to students to help build meaning. For example, say: **We can name the colors we see (brown, gray, white), but that doesn't tell us much about how we can learn about the fossils. Maybe we can find out about the fossils' ages.**	Acknowledge any response. For example, if "Will the fossils change colors?" is chosen, say: **It would be interesting to find out if the fossils change colors.** Guide students to the answer: "How old are the fossils?" **I would like to know how old the fossils are. How about you?** On the KWHL chart, record this response in the "Want (W)" column.

Investigate and describe relationships

STEP 5

Materials	Procedure	Follow-up
• Fossils: bone, fish, arrowhead • KWHL chart • Student Response Guide, page 46: **How can we find out?**	While pointing to the "W" column on the KWHL chart, restate: **We want to know how scientists learn about how old fossils are.** Then ask: **How can we find out?** Have each student respond orally, use an AAC device to respond, point to a response on the Student Response Guide page, or pantomime a digging action.	If students give alternate correct answers or incorrect answers, give a brief demo or explanation. For example, if they answer "Touch the fossils" or "Watch the fossils," you might let them touch and watch and say: **That didn't give us much information. What else should we do?** After several students respond, acknowledge the one who answers "Dig into the Earth's layers to find the fossils," or point to the preferred response and say: **I think the easiest way to find out is to dig into the Earth's layers to find them.** On the KWHL chart, record responses in the "How (H)" column. Circle "Dig into the Earth's layers to find the fossils."

Investigate and describe relationships

STEP 6		
Materials	**Procedure**	**Follow-up**
<ul><li>Model of Earth's layers</li><li>KWHL chart</li><li>Safety Rules for Science Class poster</li><li>Student Response Guide, page 47: **What do you think will happen?**</li></ul>	Review the safety rules for science listed on the poster. Say: **We learned that the Earth is made of layers. We have also learned that fossils are old and can be found in the layers. We'll use the model of the layers of the Earth and dig out fossils that are in the layers. Then we'll record which fossils we find in the layers.** **Do you think scientists can find out how old a fossil is—yes or no?**	
	Have each student make a prediction by responding orally, using an AAC device to respond, pointing to a response on the Student Response Guide page, or nodding.	Tally the students' answers—how many said yes and how many said no—and record them in the open area at the bottom of the KWHL chart to refer to at the end of the lesson.

Investigate and describe relationships

Materials	Procedure	Follow-up
• Model of Earth's layers • Metal spoon • Index card with recorded information • ScienceWork, page 85: **Earth's layers recording chart**	Say: **You each just made a prediction. Some of you said scientists can find out how old a fossil is and some of you said no, they can't. Let's find out.** Using the metal spoon, begin to dig into the top layer (layer 3) of the model. Give each student a chance to dig. Help students record what was found in the layer (no fossil) on the **Earth's layers recording chart.** Review the index card to find out on which day the layer was formed. Continue digging with the second layer (layer 2). Give each student a chance to dig. Dig until the arrowhead and fish are found. Help students record the findings on the **Earth's layers recording chart.** Review the index card to find out the date the layer was formed and write it on the chart. Continue digging with the bottom layer (layer 1). Give each student a chance to dig. Dig until the bone is found. Help students record the findings on the **Earth's layers recording chart.** Review the index card to find out the date the layer was formed and write it on the chart.	Describe aloud what happens (e.g., **Here's another layer and we found a fish**), and encourage the students to tell what they find and see. Be sure students with visual impairments actively participate in the experiment (e.g., by feeling the materials or by feeling the fossils found in the dig).

Investigate and describe relationships

STEP 8		
Materials	**Procedure**	**Follow-up**
<ul><li>Model of Earth's layers</li><li>The fossils found</li><li>Student Response Guide, page 48: **What's the same?**</li></ul>	Point to the materials used in the experiment and say: **Here are the materials we used in our experiment. Let's look at the model and these 2 layers—layer 1** (point to layer 1 and the bone) **and layer 2** (point to layer 2 and the fish and the arrowhead). **What's the same about these layers?** Have each student respond orally, use an AAC device to respond, or point to a response on the Student Response Guide page to say both have fossils and both are layers of the Earth. Prompt students who don't have symbol use to look at or touch the layers after another student correctly identifies that both are layers of the Earth.	Praise correct responses: **Yes, they are both layers of the Earth, and they both have fossils. That makes them the same.** If the students are not making a choice or are making an incorrect choice say: **Touch the brown layer. Touch the gray layer. They do not mix. They are layers of Earth's materials. They are both layers. They both had fossils in them. That makes them the same.**

Investigate and describe relationships

STEP 9

Materials	Procedure	Follow-up
• Model of Earth's layers • The fossils found • Student Response Guide, page 49: **What's different?**	Point to the materials used in the experiment and say: Here are the materials we used in our experiment. Let's look at the model and these 2 layers again. Here is layer 1 and the fossil we found (point to layer 1 and the bone), and here is layer 2 and the fossils we found (point to layer 2 and the fish and the arrowhead). What's different about these layers? Have each student respond orally, use an AAC device to respond, or point to a response on the Student Response Guide page to say the layers have different fossils, they have a different number of fossils, and the age of the fossils is different. Prompt students who don't have symbol use to look at or touch the fossils after another student correctly identifies that the layers have different fossils.	Praise correct responses: Yes, they are different. Layer 1 has a bone, layer 3 has no fossils, and layer 2 has 2 fossils. We also learned that the layers were formed on different days. The bone was in layer 1. Layer 1 was formed first, so it's the oldest. It's older than the fish we found in layer 2. The age of the fossils is different too. If the students are not making a choice or are making an incorrect choice, point to the materials and say: How many fossils were in layer 2? How many fossils were in layer 1? The number of fossils in the layers is different.

Construct explanation

STEP 10

Materials	Procedure	Follow-up
• Model of Earth's layers • The fossils found • Picture and word cards for layers and fossil • Student Response Guide, page 50: **What scientific discovery did we make?**	Read the scientific discovery statement once: **The Earth's layers can help us learn about a fossil's age.** Say: **The fossils were formed in the layers at different times. The layers of the Earth are formed at different times too. Some layers were formed long before the other layers. This means that they are older than others.** Put the picture and word cards for layers in front of the model and say: **This is the picture for layers, and this word says layers. Say "layers."**	
	Give students a turn to do the same (i.e., put the picture and word cards for layers in front of the model). For students who don't respond, have them put the picture card with the materials and then guide them to match the word card. Other students may be prompted to look at the model while you or a peer places the picture and word cards.	Give praise: **Yes, these are layers. The Earth's layers can help us learn about a fossil's age.**
	Repeat the process with the picture and word card for fossil. For students who don't respond, have them put the picture card in front of the fossils and then guide them to match the word card. Read the scientific discovery statement again, pointing to the words on the Student Response Guide page as you read and having the students follow along. Point to the models.	Give praise: **Yes, this is a fossil. The Earth's layers can help us learn about a fossil's age.**

Report

STEP 11

Materials	Procedure	Follow-up
• KWHL chart • Student Response Guide, pages 51–52: **What did we find out?** and **Why?**	Say: **Let's review what we learned. I asked you if you thought scientists could find out how old a fossil is.** Point to the predictions on the KWHL chart. **Some of you said yes, and some said no. When we dug into the model of the Earth's layers, we learned that some layers are older. They were formed earlier than others. We learned some layers have fossils in them. We can use the age of the Earth's layers to learn about the age of the fossils inside them. Can scientists learn how old a fossil is—yes or no?**	Praise the students and then summarize: **Good job. You found out that the Earth's layers help us learn a fossil's age. Then you showed me how to record a fossil's age.** If any students respond "no," point to the layers again. Write "Yes—scientists can tell a fossil's age" in the open area at the bottom of the KWHL chart.
	Say: **Some layers are formed before other layers. The fossil in the layer that formed first was older than the fossil in the layer formed after it. Why do some layers of the Earth look different?** Have each student respond orally, use an AAC device to respond, or point to a response on the Student Response Guide page to indicate that they were formed at different times.	Point to the model and say: **Good, you know that layers can help us learn a fossil's age because they're formed at different times.** Scaffold for those who don't respond by saying: **Look at the layers. Layers form at different times.**

Report

STEP 12		
Materials	**Procedure**	**Follow-up**
• KWHL chart • Student Response Guide, page 53: **What did we learn?**	Say: **Let's review what we learned. What can Earth's layers help us learn? The Earth's layers can help us learn a fossil's** _____. Have each student respond orally with "age," use an AAC device to respond, or point to a response on the Student Response Guide page to fill in the blank.	Say: **Earth's layers can help us learn a fossil's age.** Scaffold for students who say "name" by rephrasing the question: **What did we say about the age of a fossil?** Write "The Earth's layers can help us learn a fossil's age" in the "Learned (L)" column of the KWHL chart.

Review vocabulary

Materials: Picture and word cards for model, core, crust, layers, fossil, recycle

Procedure: Use the time-delay procedure to review each of the vocabulary words for the unit. See page 8 for the procedure.

Extend and review lesson

Read the story on page 19 in **ScienceWork** with the students. Help them apply the scientific concept they learned in this lesson to the story. Complete the exercise following the story together or send it home as homework.

Lesson 5 Recycling

Concept

Many materials can be used again. Recycle means to use again.

Background

In this lesson, students learn about reusing the Earth's resources. They learn about recycling and which types of materials can be recycled.

Preparation

Prepare for this lesson by having the recyclable and disposal items ready to explore and sort. Have students cut out the labels found in ScienceWork, page 87, in preparation for the activity.

Materials

- Picture and word cards for model, core, crust, layers, fossil, recycle
- KWHL chart
- Safety Rules for Science Class poster
- Student Response Guide, pages 54–64
- ScienceWork, pages 22–24 and 87

BRING FROM HOME

Bring throw-away items from home or used materials from the classroom: some to be sorted for recycling (e.g., plastic bottles, tin cans, newspaper, notebook paper, glass bottles, aluminum cans) and some for disposal (e.g., plastic bags, Styrofoam®, food).

Vocabulary

Review picture and sight word cards for this unit (see pages 30–32).

 **Engage**

STEP 1		
Materials	**Procedure**	**Follow-up**
Throw-away items	Engage the students by telling them: **Earth has limited resources, and we need to protect those resources. Today in science we're going to learn that we can protect the Earth by not using so many resources. Some items we use and throw away could be recycled or reused. Some cannot be recycled and have to be thrown away. These items fill our garbage dumps. Today we'll discover which items can be recycled.**	
	Show the throw-away items to the students and invite them to examine the materials for a few moments, make comments, and ask questions.	If students ask, "What are these?" say: **Good question.**

STEP 2		
Materials	**Procedure**	**Follow-up**
• Throw-away items • Student Response Guide, page 54: **What is this?**	Point to the throw-away items and ask: **What do you think all these things are? Make a guess.** Give each student a chance to guess before giving feedback. Remember, you do want students to make guesses in an inquiry lesson. Have each student respond orally with "garbage" or "used items," use an AAC device to respond, or point to responses on the Student Response Guide page. Prompt students who don't have symbol use to look at the throw-away items and to touch the pictures in the Student Response Guide. For example, say: **You're looking at items that are used. Touch the picture for used items.**	Praise correct responses. If students give an incorrect answer, say: **That's a good guess.** Then give a brief reason why the choice isn't the best response. For example for "money," say: **That's a good guess but the items are not money. They are items that are used.**

Engage

STEP 3

Materials	Procedure	Follow-up
• 3 of the throw-away items (1 made of glass, 1 made of plastic, 1 made of Styrofoam®) • KWHL chart • Student Response Guide, page 55: **What do you know?**	Point to the throw-away items and ask: **What do you know about these items?** Have the students tell something they know about the throw-aways. Have each student respond orally, use an AAC device to respond, or point to responses on the Student Response Guide page. Prompt students who don't have symbol use to look at the throw-away items and to touch the picture of the glass or plastic in the Student Response Guide. For example, say: **You're looking at a bottle. The bottle is made of glass.**	Praise correct responses. Correct inappropriate answers by giving a brief reason why the response isn't the best response. For example, if "They're cold" is chosen, say: **I don't think they feel cold. What else do you know?** On the KWHL chart, record the correct answers in the "Know (K)" column.

STEP 4

Materials	Procedure	Follow-up
• 3 of the throw-away items (1 made of glass, 1 made of plastic, 1 made of Styrofoam®) • KWHL chart • Student Response Guide, page 56: **What do you want to know?**	Point to the materials and ask: **What do you want to know about these items?** Have students tell anything they might want to know about the materials. Have students respond orally, use their AAC devices to respond, or point to responses on the Student Response Guide page. Prompt students who don't have symbol use to choose any picture response. Provide feedback to students to help build meaning.	Acknowledge any response. For example, if "How much do they weigh?" is chosen, say: **It would be interesting to find out how much the items weigh.** Guide students to the answer: "Can they be used again?" Say: **I would like to know if they can be used again. How about you?** On the KWHL chart, record this response in the "Want (W)" column.

Investigate and describe relationships

STEP 5

Materials	Procedure	Follow-up
• KWHL chart • Student Response Guide, page 57: **How can we find out?**	While pointing to the "W" column on the KWHL chart, restate: **We want to know which items we can use again.** Then ask: **How can we find out?** Have each student respond orally, use an AAC device to respond, point to a response on the Student Response Guide page, or pantomime looking closer at the items and looking at the labels.	If students give alternate correct answers or incorrect answers, give a brief demo or explanation. For example, if they answer "Weigh the items," you might let them weigh the items in their hands and say: **OK, we know this item weighs more. But we still don't know which items we can use again.** After several students respond, acknowledge the one who answers "Sort the items," "Look on the labels," and "Inspect the items." Or point to the preferred responses and say: **I think the easiest way to find out is to inspect them, look at the labels, and sort the items into piles.** On the KWHL chart, record responses in the "How (H)" column. Circle "Sort the items," "Look on the labels," and "Inspect the items."

Investigate and describe relationships

STEP 6

Materials	Procedure	Follow-up
• Throw-away items • KWHL chart • Safety Rules for Science Class poster • Student Response Guide, page 58: **What do you think will happen?**	Review the safety rules for science listed on the poster. Say: **We're going to sort these items by the materials they're made of. Then we'll look to see if there are labels on the items that say they can be recycled, which means they can be used again. Which items do you think we can use again?** Name whatever throw-away items you have. For example, say: **The plastic bottle—yes or no? The metal can—yes or no? The paper—yes or no? The glass—yes or no? The Styrofoam®—yes or no? The food— yes or no?**	
	Have each student make a prediction by responding orally, using an AAC device to respond, pointing to a response on the Student Response Guide page, or nodding.	Tally the students' answers for each item—how many said yes and how many said no— and record them in the open area at the bottom of the KWHL chart to refer to at the end of the lesson.

Investigate and describe relationships

STEP 7

Materials	Procedure	Follow-up
• Throw-away items to be sorted • ScienceWork, page 87: **Sorting labels**	Say: **You each just made a prediction. Some of you said you think (item chosen) can be used again.** Repeat with some or all of student predictions. Let's find out. Students can do this sort individually or as a group. Have students place the different sorting labels on a table. Have them place the label for garbage slightly away from the other labels. Place the throw-away items in a pile where students can access them. Then ask students to sort the items into piles based on what they are made of. For example, point to the paper and the label for paper and explain: **This item is made of paper. This is the label for paper that can be recycled. Make a pile with all the materials made from paper that can be recycled. Used newspaper and notebook paper could go into this pile. Take turns finding the paper items that can go in this pile.** Repeat for each of the sorting labels.	Describe aloud what happens (e.g., **This can is metal so it goes here**), and encourage the students to tell what they're doing (e.g., "Paper goes here"). Be sure students with visual impairments actively participate in the experiment. For example, give them an item to feel and tell what it is. Ask which pile the item would go into; give two choices if needed. Then guide the student to place the item in the correct pile. Praise students for sorting items correctly. If students sort items incorrectly, redirect them. Say, for example: **Let's look again. This bottle is made of glass. Find the label that shows glass and place the item in that pile.** If an item doesn't belong in a recyclable pile (i.e., it's garbage), state: **I don't think this fits into any recycle pile. Let's put it in the garbage pile.**

Investigate and describe relationships

STEP 8

Materials	Procedure	Follow-up
• Labeled piles of sorted items • Student Response Guide, page 59: **What's the same?**	Point to the piles and say: Here are the items you sorted into piles. What's the same about all these items? Have each student respond orally, use an AAC device to respond, or point to a response on the Student Response Guide page to say the items have all been used. Prompt students who don't have symbol use to look at or touch the symbol for used after another student correctly identifies that the items have been used.	Praise correct responses: Yes, they're all items that have been used. That makes them the same. If the students are not making a choice or are making an incorrect choice, hold up one item at a time and say: Look at the items we sorted. The glass bottle is empty. Someone used what was in it. The paper is written on. Someone used the paper. Both items have been used. That makes them the same.

STEP 9

Materials	Procedure	Follow-up
• Labeled piles of sorted items • Student Response Guide, page 60: **What's different?**	Point to the piles and say: Now look at the piles again. You sorted the items by what they are made of and put them in piles. What's different about these items? Have each student respond orally, use an AAC device to respond, or point to a response on the Student Response Guide page to say the items are made from different materials and some have different names on their labels. Prompt students who don't have symbol use to look at or touch the symbol for different names when someone says they have different names on their labels.	Praise correct responses: Yes, they are different. Some of the items are made of glass. Some are made of paper. Some are made of metal. Some are made of plastic. Some are made of materials that can't be reused so we sorted them into the garbage pile. The materials the items are made out of are all different. And the names on the labels are different too. If the students are not making a choice or are making an incorrect choice, hold up one item at a time and say: Remember, we sorted the items by what they are made of. Everything in this pile (point to the pile of plastic bottles) is made of plastic. Everything in this pile (point to the pile of glass) is made of glass. The materials are different.

Construct explanation

STEP 10

Materials	Procedure	Follow-up
• Labeled piles of sorted items • Picture and word cards for recycle • Student Response Guide, page 61: **What scientific discovery did we make?**	Read the scientific discovery statement once: **Many materials can be used again. Recycle means to use again.** Say: **Let's review what we did. We looked at all of these items to decide what they are made of. Then we looked at the labels to decide how to sort the items. The labels had symbols on them to show the materials that could be recycled. Some items are made of plastic** (point to the plastic pile). **Some items are made of metal** (point to the metal pile). **Some items are made of paper** (point to the paper pile). **Some items cannot be recycled, and they were placed in a pile called garbage. Most of the items had the recycle symbol on them. Items that are made of paper, glass, and metal can be recycled. Plastic can be recycled. Many materials can be used again. Recycling means to use again.** Put the picture and word cards for recycle in front of the piles and say: **This is the picture for recycle, and this word says recycle. Say "recycle."**	
	Give students a turn to do the same (i.e., put the picture and word cards for recycle in front of the piles). For students who don't respond, have them put the picture card in front of the materials and then guide them to match the word card. Other students may be prompted to look at the piles while you or a peer places the picture and word cards. Read the scientific discovery statement again, pointing to the words on the Student Response Guide page as you read and having the students follow along.	Give praise: **Yes, these items can be recycled. Say "recycled." When we sorted the items by the material they were made out of and placed them in front of the labels, we found out what could be recycled. Many materials can be used again. Recycle means to use again.**

Report

STEP 11

Materials	Procedure	Follow-up
• Labeled piles of sorted items • Picture and word cards for recycle • KWHL chart • Student Response Guide, pages 62–63: **What did we find out?** and **Why?**	Pull the items the students made predictions about to the front of the piles and then point to them and say: **Let's review what we learned. I asked you whether you thought each item could be used again. To use something again means to recycle.** Point to the predictions on the KWHL chart. **(Student's name) thought we could use this bottle again. When we sorted out the items by the materials they were made of, this bottle was put in the plastic pile. The plastic label has a recycling symbol on it. What did we find out? Which items can be used again? Can the plastic bottle be used again? What about this metal can? And the paper? What about the glass? And the Styrofoam®?** Have each student respond orally, use an AAC device to respond, point to a response on the Student Response Guide page, or nod yes or no.	Praise the students and then summarize: **Good, we learned that some used items can be used again. Most plastic, paper, metal, and glass can be used again. They can be recycled.** Write "Plastic—yes, metal—yes, paper—yes, glass—yes, Styrofoam®—no, food—no" in the open area at the bottom of the KWHL chart.
	Point to the items again and ask: **Why can we use them again?** Have each student respond orally, use an AAC device to respond, or point to a response on the Student Response Guide page to indicate that the items can be recycled. Ask students to point to the picture and word cards for recycle and then say "recycle."	Point to a label for recycle and say: **Yes, we can use these items again because they can be recycled. Recycle means to use again.** Scaffold for those who don't respond by saying: **Look at the label on our plastic pile. This symbol** (point to the symbol) **means recycle. What does this symbol mean?**

Report

STEP 12		
Materials	**Procedure**	**Follow-up**
• KWHL chart • Student Response Guide, page 64: **What did we learn?**	Say: **Let's review what we learned. Recycle means to _____.** Have each student respond orally with "use again," use an AAC device to respond, or point to a response on the Student Response Guide page to fill in the blank.	Say: **Yes, recycle means to reuse.** Scaffold for students who say "throw away" by rephrasing the question: **We sorted items into piles by the materials they were made out of. The items that were made of plastic, glass, paper, and metal can be used again. What does it mean to use something again?** Write "Recycle means to use again" in the "Learned (L)" column of the KWHL chart.

Review vocabulary

Materials: Picture and word cards for model, core, crust, layers, fossil, recycle

Procedure: Use the time-delay procedure to review each of the vocabulary words for the unit. See page 8 for the procedure.

Extend and review lesson

Read the story on page 22 in **ScienceWork** with the students. Help them apply the scientific concept they learned in this lesson to the story. Complete the exercise following the story together or send it home as homework.

Unit  B Biology

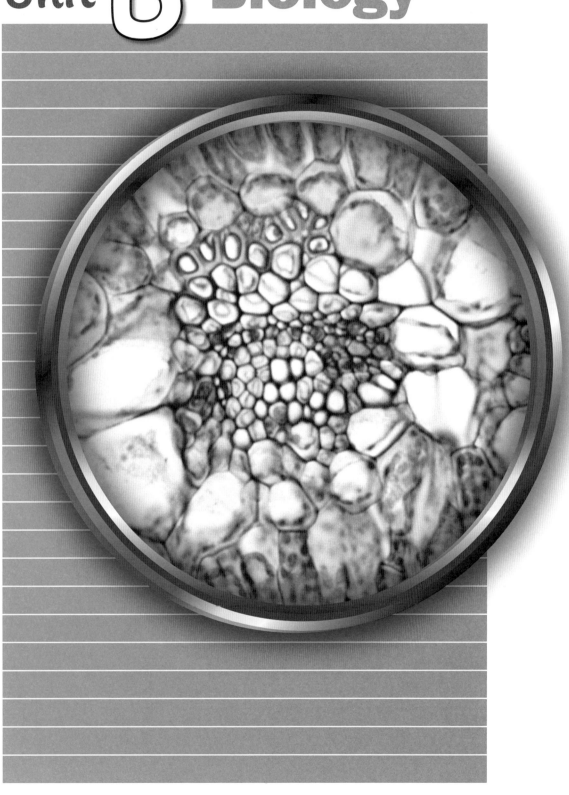

Lesson 1 Cells in living things

Concept

Living things have cells.

Background

In this lesson, students learn what a cell is and what a cell looks like. They also learn that all living things have cells, and things that are not living don't have cells. They learn that microscopes help us see cells because cells are so small.

Materials

- 2 blank slides
- Picture and word cards for cell, cell division, bacteria, disease, nutrition
- Illustration of live leaf cells and a paper leaf
- KWHL chart
- Safety Rules for Science Class poster
- Student Response Guide, pages 66–76
- ScienceWork, pages 26–29

BRING FROM HOME Plant with green leaves, green paper, microscope

Preparation

Prepare for the lesson by cutting a leaf out of green paper that is approximately the same size and shape as the live leaf. Place a piece of the paper leaf on the blank slide. Place a piece of the live leaf on the other blank slide. Prepare the microscope by focusing on the cells in the living leaf; some plant leaves have cells that are more visible under a microscope than others, so be certain to check the leaf before beginning the lesson.

Vocabulary

Teach picture symbols and sight words for this unit (see pages 82–84) to familiarize students with the vocabulary introduced in this lesson.

Engage

STEP 1		
Materials	**Procedure**	**Follow-up**
Plant	Engage the students by telling them: **Today in science we're going to learn about cells. We'll learn what a cell is. Let's begin our experiment.** Remove a leaf from the plant and set it next to the plant. **Here are some of our materials.**	
	Show the leaf and the plant to the students and invite them to examine them for a few moments, make comments, and ask questions.	If students ask, "What are these?" say: **Good question.**

STEP 2		
Materials	**Procedure**	**Follow-up**
• Plant • Leaf from plant • Student Response Guide, page 66: **What is this?**	Hold up the plant and the leaf one at a time and ask: **What do you think this is? Make a guess.** Give each student a chance to guess before giving feedback. Remember, you do want students to make guesses in an inquiry lesson. Have each student respond orally with "a plant" and "a leaf," use an AAC device to respond, or point to responses on the Student Response Guide page. Prompt students who don't have symbol use to look at the leaf and to touch the picture of the leaf in the Student Response Guide. For example, say: **You're looking at a leaf. This is a leaf.**	Praise correct responses. If students give an incorrect answer, say: **That's a good guess.** Then give a brief reason why the choice isn't the best response. For example, for "broccoli," say: **It looks like broccoli, but it's actually a leaf from a plant.**

 **Engage**

STEP 3

Materials	Procedure	Follow-up
• Leaf from plant • Paper leaf • KWHL chart • Student Response Guide, page 67: **What do you know?**	Point to the plant leaf and ask: **What do you know about this leaf?** Have the students tell something they know about the plant leaf. Have each student respond orally, use an AAC device to respond, or point to responses on the Student Response Guide page. Prompt students who don't have symbol use to look at the plant leaf and to touch the picture of living in the Student Response Guide. For example, say: **You're looking at the leaf. It's living.**	Praise correct responses. Correct inappropriate answers by giving a brief reason why the response isn't the best response. For example, if "It plays tennis" is chosen, say: **I don't think a leaf plays tennis. People play tennis, but leaves do not. This leaf is a part of a living plant, and it's green.** On the KWHL chart, record the correct answers in the "Know (K)" column.
	Introduce the paper leaf. Say: **This is another leaf, but it's not real. It's paper. This paper leaf is not alive.** Encourage students to touch both leaves and identify the one that's living.	Praise correct responses: **Great, you found the living leaf.**

STEP 4

Materials	Procedure	Follow-up
• Leaf from plant • Paper leaf • Microscope • KWHL chart • Student Response Guide, page 68: **What do you want to know?**	Introduce the microscope to the students. Say: **This is a microscope. We use microscopes in science to see things that are too small to see with our eyes alone. It will magnify the little things we want to see. What do you want to know about these leaves and this microscope?** Have students tell anything they might want to know about the materials. Have students respond orally, use their AAC devices to respond, or point to responses on the Student Response Guide page. Prompt students who don't have symbol use to choose any picture response. Provide feedback to students to help build meaning.	Acknowledge any response. For example, if "Will the leaves disappear under the microscope?" is chosen, say: **It would be interesting to find out if the leaves will disappear under the microscope.** Guide students to the answer: "What do the leaves look like under the microscope?" Say: **I would like to know what the leaves look like under the microscope. How about you?** On the KWHL chart, record this response in the "Want (W)" column.

Investigate and describe relationships

STEP 5

Materials	Procedure	Follow-up
• KWHL chart • Student Response Guide, page 69: **How can we find out?**	While pointing to the "W" column on the KWHL chart, restate: We want to know what the leaves look like under the microscope. Then ask: How can we find out? Have each student respond orally, use an AAC device to respond, point to a response on the Student Response Guide page, or pantomime looking into a microscope.	If students give alternate correct answers or incorrect answers, give a brief demo or explanation. For example, if they answer "Listen to the leaves," let them listen to the leaves and say: That didn't give us much information. What else could we do? After several students respond, acknowledge the one who answers "Put the leaves under the microscope," or point to the preferred response and say: I think the easiest way to find out is to put the leaves under the microscope and look at them. On the KWHL chart, record responses in the "How (H)" column. Circle "put the leaves under the microscope."

STEP 6

Materials	Procedure	Follow-up
• Leaf from plant • Paper leaf • Microscope • Illustration of live leaf cells and paper leaf • KWHL chart • Safety Rules for Science Class poster • Student Response Guide, page 70: **What do you think will happen?**	Review the safety rules for science listed on the poster. Introduce the concept of a cell. Show the students the illustration of the leaf cells. Say: This is an picture of cells. Cells are the smallest parts of living things. They are so small that you can see them only with a microscope. Here are two leaves. One is from a plant, and the other is made of paper. I wonder if we use this microscope to look at the leaves closer, whether you'll see cells in these leaves. Which leaf do you think will have cells? The paper leaf or the plant leaf?	
	Have each student make a prediction by responding orally, using an AAC device to respond, pointing to a response on the Student Response Guide page, or pointing to one of the leaves.	Tally the students' answers—how many said the paper leaf and how many said the plant leaf—and record them in the open area at the bottom of the KWHL chart to refer to at the end of the lesson.

Investigate and describe relationships

STEP 7

Materials	Procedure	Follow-up
• Illustration of live leaf cells and paper leaf • Leaf from plant • Paper leaf • Microscope • 2 prepared slides	Say: **You just made a prediction. Some of you said you thought you would see the cells in the leaf from the plant, and some of you said you would see cells in the paper leaf. Let's find out.** Have one student put the slide with the living cells under the microscope. Guide the student to describe what he or she sees (small ovals or cells); or using the illustration of the live leaf cells and the paper leaf, have the student point to the leaf picture that looks like what he or she saw under the microscope. Help each student look into the microscope and point to the illustration of the live leaf cells. Say: **In the leaf from the plant, we saw a lot of small ovals. These are all plant cells. We saw cells in the leaf from a plant. Do you remember what we said we know about this leaf? We said it was living.** Repeat with the paper leaf. Compare the paper leaf to the living cells in the plant leaf. Say: **In the paper leaf, we do not see small ovals or cells. We see only small lines. This leaf does not have cells. It is not living.**	Describe aloud what the students are seeing, and encourage them to tell what they see (e.g., "small circles" or "small ovals") in the microscope. Be sure students with visual impairments actively participate in the experiment (e.g., cut out of paper small ovals and have students place them onto the illustration of the live leaf cells).

Investigate and describe relationships

STEP 8

Materials	Procedure	Follow-up
• Leaf from plant • Paper leaf • Illustration of live leaf cells and paper leaf • Student Response Guide, page 71: **What's the same?**	Place the plant leaf next to the illustration of the live leaf cells. Point to the plant leaf and the illustration and say: **Here's one material from the experiment.** Point to the paper leaf and say: **Here's another material from the experiment. What's the same about both of the materials?** Have each student respond orally, use an AAC device to respond, or point to a response on the Student Response Guide page to say they are both leaves and both green. Prompt students who don't have symbol use to look at or touch the leaves after another student correctly identifies that the materials are both leaves and both green.	Praise correct responses: **Yes, they are both leaves and both green. That makes them the same.** If the students are not making a choice or are making an incorrect choice, hold up both leaves and say: **What are both of these items? They're both leaves. That makes them the same.**

STEP 9

Materials	Procedure	Follow-up
• Leaf from plant • Paper leaf • Illustration of live leaf cells and paper leaf • Student Response Guide, page 72: **What's different?**	Point to the plant leaf and say: **Here's one material from the experiment.** Point to the paper leaf and say: **Here's another material from the experiment. What's different about these materials?** Have each student respond orally, use an AAC device to respond, or point to a response on the Student Response Guide page to say one is living and one has cells. Prompt students who don't have symbol use to look at or touch the plant leaf after another student correctly identifies that the plant leaf is living and has cells.	Praise correct responses: **Yes, one leaf is living and has cells, and the other doesn't have cells so it's not living. That makes them different.** If the students are not making a choice or are making an incorrect choice, say: **Let's look at the picture of the live leaf cells. When we looked at the plant leaf, we saw all these small oval cells. But when we looked at the paper leaf in the microscope, we did not see the cells. We only saw little lines. They did not both have cells. Only one leaf was living. It had cells. That makes them different.**

Construct explanation

STEP 10

Materials	Procedure	Follow-up
• Picture and word cards for cell • Student Response Guide, page 73: **What scientific discovery did we make?**	Read the scientific discovery statement once: **Living things have cells.** Say: **Let's review what we did. First we looked at a plant leaf under the microscope and saw that it had cells like the picture** (point to the illustration). **It was living. It had cells.** Then hold up the picture and word cards for cell and say: **This is the picture for cell, and this word says cell. Say "cell."** Put the picture and word cards for cell in front of the illustration of the live leaf cells.	
	Give students a turn to do the same (i.e., put the picture and word cards in front of the illustration of the live leaf cells). For students who don't respond, have them put the picture card with the materials and then guide them to match the word card. Other students may be prompted to look at the illustration while you or a peer places the picture and word cards. Read the scientific discovery statement again, pointing to the words on the Student Response Guide page as you read and having the students follow along.	Give praise: **Yes, this is a cell. Say "cell."**

Report

STEP 11		
Materials	**Procedure**	**Follow-up**
• Picture and word cards for cell • KWHL chart • Student Response Guide, pages 74–75: **What did we find out?** and **Why?**	Say: **Let's review what we learned. I asked you which leaf you thought would have cells.** Point to the predictions on the KWHL chart. **Some of you said the leaf from the plant, and some of you said you would see cells in the paper leaf. In which leaf did you find cells?** Have each student respond orally, use an AAC device to respond, point to a response on the Student Response Guide page, or nod yes or no as you hold up the plant leaf.	Praise the students and then summarize: **Good, we saw in the microscope that the leaf from the plant had cells. We know that the leaf is living. Living things have cells. The leaf from the plant had little oval cells** (point to the illustration of the live leaf). If any students respond "paper leaf," show the illustration of the plant leaf again and say: **The plant is living and has cells.** Write "Leaf from plant has cells" in the open area at the bottom of the KWHL chart.
	Point to the plant leaf and ask: **Why did the leaf from the plant have cells?** Have each student respond orally, use an AAC device to respond, or point to a response on the Student Response Guide page to indicate that the leaf had cells because it was living. Ask students to point to the picture and word cards for cell and then say "cell."	Point to the plant leaf and say: **Yes, when we looked into the microscope and saw the small oval cells in the leaf from the plant, we learned that this leaf is living.** Scaffold for those who don't respond by asking: **What do we know about a leaf with cells?**

Report

STEP 12		
Materials	**Procedure**	**Follow-up**
• KWHL chart • Student Response Guide, page 76: **What did we learn?**	Say: **Let's review what we learned. Living things** _____. Have each student respond orally with "have cells," use an AAC device to respond, or point to a response on the Student Response Guide page to fill in the blank.	Say: **Yes, living things have cells.** Scaffold for students who say "do not have cells" by pointing to the illustration of the live leaf cells and saying: **This is a living thing. What do you see—cells or no cells?** Write "Plant leaf cells = living" in the "Learned (L)" column of the KWHL chart.

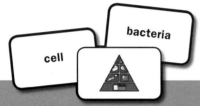

Teach vocabulary

Materials	Procedure	Follow-up
Picture cards: • cell • cell division • bacteria • disease • nutrition	Review the picture cards with students individually when possible. In this first round, give the student a prompt without delay (zero time delay). Place the picture cards in front of the student. Say: **Show me (cell)** and point to the card as you ask the student to point (zero time delay). Shuffle the cards. Repeat this procedure for the remaining 4 cards.	If the student points correctly, give praise: **Good! You pointed to (cell). Say (cell).** If the student doesn't point, provide physical guidance to point.
	In this second round of vocabulary review, give the student up to 5 seconds to respond independently (5-second time delay). Shuffle the picture cards, place them in front of the student, and say: **Point to (cell).** Repeat this process for the remaining 4 cards.	If the student points correctly, give praise: **Good! You pointed to (cell) by yourself. Say (cell).** If the student doesn't point, model pointing and say: **This is (cell). Point to (cell). Say (cell).** If the student makes an error, point to the correct answer and say: **This is (cell). Point to (cell). Say (cell).** Shuffle the cards and repeat this process for the remaining 4 cards.

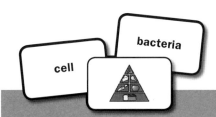

Teach vocabulary

Materials	Procedure	Follow-up
Word cards: • cell • cell division • bacteria • disease • nutrition	Review the word cards with students individually if possible. In this first round, give the student a prompt without delay (zero time delay). Place the word cards in front of the student. Say: **Show me (cell)** and point to the card as you ask the student to point (zero time delay). Shuffle the cards. Repeat this procedure for the remaining 4 cards.	If the student points correctly, give praise: **Good! You pointed to (cell). Say (cell).** If the student doesn't point, provide physical guidance to point.
	In this second round of vocabulary review, give the student up to 5 seconds to respond independently (5-second time delay). Shuffle the word cards, place them in front of the student, and say: **Point to (cell).** Repeat this process for the remaining 4 cards.	If the student points correctly, give praise: **Good! You pointed to (cell) by yourself. Say (cell).** If the student doesn't point, model pointing and say: **This is (cell). Point to (cell). Say (cell).** If the student makes an error, point to the correct answer and say: **This is (cell). Point to (cell). Say (cell).** Shuffle the cards and repeat this process for the remaining 4 cards.

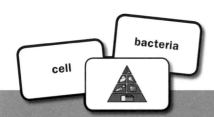

Teach vocabulary

Materials	Procedure	Follow-up
Picture and word cards: • cell • cell division • bacteria • disease • nutrition	In the first round, place the word cards in front of the student. Then hand a picture card to the student and say: **Match this picture to the word.** Match the picture card to the word card as you ask the student to match them (zero time delay). Shuffle the cards. Repeat this procedure for the remaining 4 cards.	If the student matches correctly, give praise: **Good! You matched the picture to the word. Say (cell).** If the student doesn't match the cards, provide physical guidance to point.
	In a second round, give the student up to 5 seconds to match 2 cards independently (5-second time delay). Repeat this process for the remaining 4 cards.	If the student matches correctly, give praise: **Good! You matched the two cards by yourself. Say (cell).** If the student doesn't match the cards, model matching and say: **This is (cell). Match this card to the word (cell). Say (cell).** If the student makes an error, point to the correct answer and say: **This is (cell). Match this card to (cell). Say (cell).** Shuffle the cards and repeat this process for the remaining 4 cards.

Reviewing vocabulary in a group

If reviewing vocabulary in a group, follow the format described, but have one student respond while you cue the others to watch. Pick a second student at random to repeat the response from time to time to be sure everyone is watching.

Extend and review lesson

Read the story on pages 26–27 in **ScienceWork** with the students. Help them apply the scientific concept they learned in this lesson to the story. Complete the exercise following the story together or send it home as homework.

Lesson 2 Parts of a cell

Concept

Cells have parts.

Background

In this lesson, students learn about the parts of a cell. They're introduced to the basic parts of a cell (the nucleus, the cell wall, and the cytoplasm), and they compare two types of cells (an onion cell and an animal cell). Finally, they review that cells are too small to see with the eyes, but a microscope can help see the inside of a cell. You may need to review how to use a microscope.

Materials

- Onion skin slide
- Measuring cup
- Metal spoon
- Picture and word cards for cell, cell division, bacteria, disease, nutrition
- Illustration of plant cell and animal cell
- KWHL chart
- Safety Rules for Science Class poster
- Student Response Guide, pages 77–87
- ScienceWork, pages 30–33

BRING FROM HOME Onion, zip-tight plastic sandwich bag, box of gelatin, grape, microscope

Preparation

Prepare a model of an onion cell, using the zip-tight plastic bag and the gelatin. Pour the gelatin in the measuring cup. Add 1 cup of hot water to the gelatin and stir with the metal spoon. When the gelatin thickens, add it to the plastic zip-tight bag. The wall of the bag is the cell wall, and the gelatin replicates the cytoplasm.

Focus the microscope on the onion skin slide. Make sure cell parts are visible and focused.

Vocabulary

Review picture and sight word cards for this unit (see pages 82–84).

Engage

STEP 1		
Materials	**Procedure**	**Follow-up**
• Microscope • Onion skin slide	Engage the students by telling them: **Today in science we're going to learn more about cells. We'll learn about what a cell looks like inside. Let's begin our experiment. Here are some of our materials.**	
	Point to the microscope and the onion skin slide. Invite the students to examine them for a few moments, make comments, and ask questions.	If students ask, "What are these?" say: **Good question.**

STEP 2		
Materials	**Procedure**	**Follow-up**
• Microscope • Onion skin slide • Student Response Guide, page 77: **What is this?**	Point to the microscope and ask: **What do you think this is? Make a guess.** Give each student a chance to guess before giving feedback. Remember, you do want students to make guesses in an inquiry lesson. Have each student respond orally with "a microscope," use an AAC device to respond, or point to responses on the Student Response Guide page. Prompt students who don't have symbol use to look at the microscope and to touch the picture of the microscope in the Student Response Guide. For example, say: **You're looking at a microscope. This is a microscope.** Repeat this process with the slide of the onion skin and tell students that the slide has a cell from an onion on it.	Praise correct responses. If students give an incorrect answer, say: **That's a good guess.** Then give a brief reason why the choice isn't the best response. For example, for "a computer," say: **It looks a little like a computer, but it's actually a microscope.**

Engage

STEP 3

Materials	Procedure	Follow-up
<ul><li>Microscope</li><li>Onion</li><li>Onion skin slide</li><li>KWHL chart</li><li>Student Response Guide, page 78: **What do you know?**</li></ul>	First point to the onion and then to the onion skin slide and ask: **What do you know about the cells on this slide?** Have the students tell something they know about the slide. Have each student respond orally, use an AAC device to respond, or point to responses on the Student Response Guide page. Prompt students who don't have symbol use to look at the slide and to touch the picture of "They're small" in the Student Response Guide. For example, say: **You're looking at the slide. It shows us small cells.**	Praise correct responses. Correct inappropriate answers by giving a brief reason why the response isn't the best response. For example, if "They have bubbles" is chosen, say: **I don't think the cells have bubbles. Look at the slide. I don't see any bubbles.** On the KWHL chart, record the correct answers in the "Know (K)" column.

STEP 4

Materials	Procedure	Follow-up
<ul><li>Onion skin slide</li><li>Onion</li><li>Microscope</li><li>KWHL chart</li><li>Student Response Guide, page 79: **What do you want to know?**</li></ul>	Hold up the onion and the onion skin slide and say: **This is an onion and this is a slide. There are many cells on this slide. What do you want to know about a cell of an onion skin on this slide?** Have students tell anything they might want to know about the slide and the onion cell. Have students respond orally, use their AAC devices to respond, or point to responses on the Student Response Guide page. Prompt students who don't have symbol use to choose any picture response. Provide feedback to students to help build meaning.	Acknowledge any response. For example, if "Will the cell grow?" is chosen, say: **It would be interesting to find out if a cell will grow.** Guide students to the answer: "What does the inside of a cell look like?" Say: **I would like to know what the inside of a cell looks like under this microscope. How about you?** On the KWHL chart, record this response in the "Want (W)" column.

Investigate and describe relationships

STEP 5

Materials	Procedure	Follow-up
• Onion skin slide • Microscope • KWHL chart • Student Response Guide, page 80: **How can we find out?**	While pointing to the "W" column on the KWHL chart, restate: **We want to know what the inside of a cell looks like under this microscope.** Then ask: **How can we find out?** Have each student respond orally, use an AAC device to respond, point to a response on the Student Response Guide page, or pantomime looking into a microscope.	If students give alternate correct answers or incorrect answers, give a brief demo or explanation. For example, if they answer "Touch the slide," let them touch the slide and say: **That didn't give us much information. What else could we do?** After several students respond, acknowledge the one who answers, "Look in the microscope," or point to the preferred response and say: **I think the easiest way to see the inside of an onion cell is to use the microscope. A cell is so small that we can't see it with our eyes. We'll have to use this microscope to make it larger to see.** On the KWHL chart, record responses in the "How (H)" column. Circle "Look in the microscope."

Investigate and describe relationships

STEP 6

Materials	Procedure	Follow-up
• Onion skin slide • Microscope • KWHL chart • Safety Rules for Science Class poster • Student Response Guide, page 81: **What do you think will happen?**	Review the safety rules for science listed on the poster. Place the slide under the microscope and focus it. Say: **We know that we need to use the microscope to see an onion's cell. Cells are the smallest parts of living things. They are so small that you can see them only with a microscope. We'll look into the microscope to see the cells up close. What do you think a cell will look like under the microscope? Will it have parts or be whole with no parts?**	
	Have each student make a prediction by responding orally, using an AAC device to respond, pointing to a response on the Student Response Guide page, or nodding when you say "has parts" or "is whole with no parts."	Tally the students' answers—how many said a cell has parts and how many said a cell is whole with no parts—and record them in the open area at the bottom of the KWHL chart to refer to at the end of the lesson.

Investigate and describe relationships

STEP 7

Materials	Procedure	Follow-up
<ul><li>Onion skin slide</li><li>Microscope</li><li>Model of onion cell</li><li>Grape</li><li>Illustration of plant cell and animal cell</li></ul>	Say: **You just made a prediction. Some of you said a cell will have parts, and some of you said a cell will be whole with no parts. Let's find out.** Have one student put the onion skin slide under the microscope and look into it. Guide the student to describe what he or she sees: a dark, round area (the nucleus); the outside layer (the cell wall); and the cytoplasm (the fluid the nucleus is in). Give each student a turn to look into the microscope. Say: **The dark, round part inside a cell is called the nucleus, the outside layer is called the cell wall, and the fluid the nucleus is in is called the cytoplasm.** Help each student look into the microscope to see the nucleus, the cell wall, and the cytoplasm.	Describe aloud what the students are seeing. Encourage the students to tell what they see (e.g., "small circles in the cells") in the microscope. Be sure students with visual impairments actively participate in the experiment (e.g., by placing the grape into the model of the onion cell).
	Hold up the onion cell model (the zip-tight bag filled with the gelatin). Have one student add the grape to the bag and explain: **We're adding this grape to the bag to create a model of an onion cell. The outside of the bag is the cell wall. The grape is the nucleus of the cell. The jelly is the cytoplasm. See how the onion cell has several parts. This cell model looks like the cell we saw in the microscope. Let's name the parts.** Point to the nucleus, the cell wall, and the cytoplasm, and name the parts.	

(Step continues)

Investigate and describe relationships

	STEP 7—*Continued*	
Materials	**Procedure**	**Follow-up**
	Introduce students to the illustration of the plant cell and the animal cell. Say: **Here's what a plant cell looks like and what an animal cell looks like. Notice that the animal cell also has parts. It has different parts than the plant cell.** Have each student point to the nucleus, the cell wall, and then to the cytoplasm on the plant cell as you say the parts. Note that the animal cell does not have a cell wall; rather, it has a cell membrane.	

	STEP 8	
Materials	**Procedure**	**Follow-up**
• Model of onion cell • Illustration of plant cell and animal cell • Student Response Guide, page 82: **What's the same?**	Point to the illustration of the animal cell and the model of the onion cell and say: **Look at both cells. This one is a model of the onion cell, and this is an animal cell. What's the same about both of these cells?** Have each student respond orally, use an AAC device to respond, or point to a response on the Student Response Guide page to say both have parts and both come from living things. Prompt students who don't have symbol use to look at or touch the parts of the cell on the model or on the illustration after another student correctly identifies that both have parts.	Praise correct responses: **Yes, both cells have parts. That makes them the same.** If the students are not making a choice or are making an incorrect choice, guide them by saying: **Let's point to the parts in the onion cell. Now let's point to the parts in the animal cell. Great job. You pointed to the parts. Both cells have parts, and both cells are from living things.**

Investigate and describe relationships

	STEP 9	
Materials	**Procedure**	**Follow-up**
• Illustration of plant cell and animal cell • Student Response Guide, page 83: **What's different?**	Point to the illustration of the plant cell and the animal cell and say: **Now look at both of the cells again. What's different about these cells?** Have each student respond orally, use an AAC device to respond, or point to a response on the Student Response Guide page to say one is from a plant. Prompt students who don't have symbol use to look at or touch the onion cell after another student correctly identifies that one cell is from a plant.	Praise correct responses: **Yes, one cell is from a plant—an onion—and the other is from an animal. That makes them different.** If the students are not making a choice or are making an incorrect choice, say: **Where is this cell from?** Point to the onion cell. **Yes, it's from an onion.** Point to the animal cell. **Yes, and this is from an animal. The cells are from different living things.**

Construct explanation

STEP 10

Materials	Procedure	Follow-up
<ul><li>Model of onion cell</li><li>Picture and word cards for cell</li><li>Illustration of plant cell and animal cell</li><li>Student Response Guide, page 84: **What scientific discovery did we make?**</li></ul>	Read the scientific discovery statement once: Cells have parts. Say: Let's review what we did. First we looked at onion cells on the slide under the microscope. Then we made a model of an onion cell (point to the model). The model has a nucleus, a cell wall, and cytoplasm. Then I showed you a picture of an animal cell, and we saw that it also had parts. It has a nucleus, a cell membrane, and cytoplasm. Then hold up the picture and word cards for cell and say: This is the picture for cell and this word says cell. Say "cell." Put the picture and word cards for cell in front of the model of the onion cell.	
	Give students a turn to do the same (i.e., put the picture and word cards in front of the onion cell model). For students who don't respond, have them put the picture card in front of the cell model and then guide them to match the word card. Other students may be prompted to look at the model of the cell while you or a peer places the picture and word cards. Read the scientific discovery statement again, pointing to the words on the Student Response Guide page as you read and having the students follow along.	Give praise: Yes, this is a cell. Say "cell."

Report

STEP 11

Materials	Procedure	Follow-up
• Onion • Model of onion cell • Picture and word cards for cell • KWHL chart • Student Response Guide, pages 85–86: **What did we find out?** and **Why?**	Say: **Let's review what we learned. I asked you what you thought a cell would look like under the microscope.** Point to the predictions on the KWHL chart. **Some of you said a cell would have parts. Some of you said a cell would be whole and not have parts. Does a cell have parts or not?** Have each student respond orally, use an AAC device to respond, point to a response on the Student Response Guide page, or nod yes or no as you say "had parts" or "was whole with no parts."	Praise the students and then summarize: **Good, we looked at the inside of cells in the microscope. Then we made a model of a cell. We saw the onion cell parts: a nucleus, a cell wall, and cytoplasm. The onion cell had parts, and the animal cell had parts. We learned that cells have parts.** If any students respond "no parts," show the model of the onion cell and say: **The cell has parts—a nucleus, a cell wall, and cytoplasm.** Write "Cells have parts" in the open area at the bottom of the KWHL chart.
	Point to the onion cell model and ask: **Why does a cell have parts?** Have each student respond orally, use an AAC device to respond, or point to a response on the Student Response Guide page to indicate that a cell has parts because it's from a living thing. Ask students to point to the picture and word cards for cell and then say "cell."	Point to the onion and say: **Yes, when we looked into the microscope we saw that the cells had parts and that's because cells are in living things.** Scaffold for those who don't respond by asking: **When you looked in the microscope, you saw different parts of a cell. What things have cells with parts?**

Report

STEP 12		
Materials	**Procedure**	**Follow-up**
• Model of onion cell • KWHL chart • Student Response Guide, page 87 **What did we learn?**	Say: **Let's review what we learned. Cells have _____.** Have each student respond orally with "parts," use an AAC device to respond, or point to a response on the Student Response Guide page to fill in the blank.	Say: **Yes, cells have parts.** Scaffold for students who say "layers" or "headaches" by pointing to the cell model and saying: **This is the nucleus, and this is the cell wall. Cells have parts.** Write "Cells have parts" in the "Learned (L)" column of the KWHL chart.

Review vocabulary

Materials: Picture and word cards for cell, cell division, bacteria, disease, nutrition

Procedure: Use the time-delay procedure to review each of the vocabulary words for the unit. See page 8 for the procedure.

Extend and review lesson

Read the story on pages 30–31 in **ScienceWork** with the students. Help them apply the scientific concept they learned in this lesson to the story. Complete the exercise following the story together or send it home as homework.

Lesson 3   **Cell division**

Concept

Cell division makes living things grow.

Background

In this lesson, students learn that cells divide. They also learn the role cell division has in the growth process of living things.

Materials

- Play-Doh® in 3 colors
- Picture and word cards for cell, cell division, bacteria, disease, nutrition
- KWHL chart
- Safety Rules for Science Class poster
- Student Response Guide, pages 88–98
- ScienceWork, pages 34–36

BRING FROM HOME

Rolling pin

TO REPLENISH MATERIALS

In this experiment, you can use any pliable clay or Play-Doh®. Create your own play dough using the following recipe:

- 1 cup flour
- 1 cup warm water
- 2 teaspoons cream of tartar
- 1 teaspoon oil
- ¼ cup salt
- food coloring

Mix all ingredients, adding food coloring last. Stir over medium heat until smooth. Remove from pan and knead until blended smooth.

Preparation

Prepare two models of cells. Roll out one color of Play-Doh® to form two 4" x 6" rectangles. Roll a second color into a rope and use it to frame the rectangles (i.e., the cell wall). Form 2 balls about 1" in diameter using the third color; flatten them to form the nuclei. Place in the centers of the rectangles.

Vocabulary

Review picture and sight word cards for this unit (see pages 82–84).

 Engage

STEP 1		
Materials	**Procedure**	**Follow-up**
Cell models	Engage the students by telling them: **Today in science we're going to learn more about cells. We'll learn more about living things. Let's begin our experiment. Here are some of our materials.**	
	Point to the two cell models. Invite the students to examine them for a few moments, make comments, and ask questions.	If students ask, "What are these?" say: **Good question.**

STEP 2		
Materials	**Procedure**	**Follow-up**
• Cell models • Student Response Guide, page 88: **What is this?**	Point to the cell models and ask: **What do you think these are? Make a guess.** Give each student a chance to guess before giving feedback. Remember, you do want students to make guesses in an inquiry lesson. Have each student respond orally with "models," use an AAC device to respond, or point to responses on the Student Response Guide page. Prompt students who don't have symbol use to look at the models and to touch the picture of models in the Student Response Guide. For example, say: **You're looking at models of plant cells. These are models of plant cells.**	Praise correct responses. If students give an incorrect answer, say: **That's a good guess.** Then give a brief reason why the choice isn't the best response. For example, for "pizzas," say: **They look a little like pizzas, but they're models of plant cells.**

Engage

STEP 3

Materials	Procedure	Follow-up
<ul><li>Cell models</li><li>KWHL chart</li><li>Student Response Guide, page 89: **What do you know?**</li></ul>	Point to the models and say: **Today we'll learn more about living things. We'll use these models of plant cells. These cells are like the ones we saw under the microscope.** Then ask: **What do you know about these models?** Have the students tell something they know about the models. Have each student respond orally, use an AAC device to respond, or point to responses on the Student Response Guide page. Prompt students who don't have symbol use to look at the models and to touch the picture of "They're models of cells" in the Student Response Guide. For example, say: **You're looking at models of plant cells. We saw real plant cells under a microscope in another lesson.**	Praise correct responses. Point to the cell parts on the models and say: **Yes, these cells have parts.** Correct inappropriate answers by giving a brief reason why the response isn't the best response. For example, if "They're loud" is chosen, say: **I don't think I can hear anything. Let's listen. The cells are not loud.** On the KWHL chart, record the correct answers in the "Know (K)" column.

STEP 4

Materials	Procedure	Follow-up
<ul><li>Cell models</li><li>KWHL chart</li><li>Student Response Guide, page 90: **What do you want to know?**</li></ul>	Point to the models and say: **These are models of plant cells. What do you want to know about these cells?** Have students tell anything they might want to know about the models of cells. Have students respond orally, use their AAC devices to respond, or point to responses on the Student Response Guide page. Prompt students who don't have symbol use to choose any picture response. Provide feedback to students to help build meaning.	Acknowledge any response. For example, if "Is a cell cold?" is chosen, say: **It would be interesting to find out if the cells are cold.** Guide students to the answer: "How do cells make living things grow?" Say: **I would like to know how cells make living things grow. How about you?** On the KWHL chart, record this response in the "Want (W)" column.

Investigate and describe relationships

STEP 5

Materials	Procedure	Follow-up
• Cell models • KWHL chart • Student Response Guide, page 91: **How can we find out?**	While pointing to the "W" column on the KWHL chart, restate: **We want to know how cells make living things grow.** Then ask: **How can we find out?** Have each student respond orally, use an AAC device to respond, point to a response on the Student Response Guide page, or pantomime touching the cell parts.	If a student gives alternate correct answers or incorrect answers, give a brief demo or explanation. For example, if they answer "Listen to the cells," listen for a moment and say: **That didn't give us much information. What else could we do?** After several students respond, acknowledge the one who answers, "Look at the cell models," or point to the preferred response and say: **I think the easiest way to see how cells make living things grow is to look at the cell models.** On the KWHL chart, record responses in the "How (H)" column. Circle "Look at the cell models."

STEP 6

Materials	Procedure	Follow-up
• Cell models • KWHL chart • Safety Rules for Science Class poster • Student Response Guide, page 92: **What do you think will happen?**	Review the safety rules for science listed on the poster. Point to the cell models and say: **We'll use the cell models to learn what cells do to make living things grow. What do you think cells do to make living things grow? Do they divide or do they stay together?**	
	Have each student make a prediction by responding orally, using an AAC device to respond, pointing to a response on the Student Response Guide page, or nodding when you say "divide" or "stay together."	Tally the students' answers—how many said cells divide and how many said cells stay together—and record them in the open area at the bottom of the KWHL chart to refer to at the end of the lesson.

Investigate and describe relationships

STEP 7

Materials	Procedure	Follow-up
Cell models	Say: **You just made a prediction. Some of you said cells divide, and some of you said cells do not divide, but stay together. Let's find out.** Point to one of the cell models and draw attention to the cell parts. Say: **Here's a cell with a cell wall, cytoplasm, and a nucleus. We'll keep this cell just the way it is.** Point to the other cell model. Draw attention to the cell parts. Say: **Here's another cell with a cell wall, cytoplasm, and a nucleus. This cell model will divide apart. To divide means to break something into pieces.** Have a student help you pinch the cell wall, squeezing it from top to bottom and going through the nucleus to divide the cell into 2 equal cells. If needed, remold the cell wall and nucleus to make 2 equal cells. Say: **I divided 1 cell into 2 equal cells. Now, each of these new cells will divide in the same way.** Next, have a student help you use the same process to divide each of the 2 new cells to make a total of 4 new cells. If needed, remold the cell walls and nuclei to make 4 equal cells. Say: **The cells divided again to make 4 cells.**	Describe aloud what you're doing. Encourage the students to tell what they see (e.g., "Now there's 2"). Be sure students with visual impairments actively participate in the experiment (e.g., by feeling that one cell model stays together and the other cell model divides into 4 equal-sized cells).

Investigate and describe relationships

STEP 8

Materials	Procedure	Follow-up
• Cell models • Student Response Guide, page 93: **What's the same?**	Point to the cell model that was not divided and the multiple cells and say: **Here are the models we used in our experiment. What's the same about these models?** Have each student respond orally, use an AAC device to respond, or point to a response on the Student Response Guide page to say both are models of plant cells and both have parts. Prompt students who don't have symbol use to look at or touch the model after another student correctly identifies that both are models of plant cells and both have parts.	Praise correct responses: **Yes, both of these are models of plant cells, and both have parts. That makes them the same.** If the students are not making a choice or are making an incorrect choice, guide them by saying: **We have models of cells. The models are both plant cells and have the same parts. That makes them the same.**

STEP 9

Materials	Procedure	Follow-up
• Cell models • Student Response Guide, page 94: **What's different?**	Point to the cell model that was not divided and the multiple cells and say: **Now look at both of the models again. What's different about these models?** Have each student respond orally, use an AAC device to respond, or point to a response on the Student Response Guide page to say the models have a different number of cells. Prompt students who don't have symbol use to look at or touch the models after another student correctly identifies that they have a different number of cells.	Praise correct responses: **Yes, the number of cells is different. One model has just 1 cell, and the other model now has 4 cells. That makes them different.** If the students are not making a choice or are making an incorrect choice, say: **Look at each model.** Point to the models. **Let's count the number of cells in these models.** Count with the student.

Construct explanation

STEP 10

Materials	Procedure	Follow-up
<ul><li>Cell models</li><li>Picture and word cards for cell division</li><li>Student Response Guide, page 95: **What scientific discovery did we make?**</li></ul>	Read the scientific discovery statement once: **Cell division makes living things grow.** Say: **Let's review what we did. We learned that living things have cells. We also learned that cells have parts. Cell parts do something special to make living things grow. Cell parts—like the cell wall, cytoplasm, and nucleus in our plant cell models—divide and make new cells. Living things need to make more cells to keep growing. Today we learned about cell division.** Then hold up the picture and word cards for cell division and say: **This is the picture for cell division, and these words say cell division. Say "cell division."** Put the picture and word cards for cell division in front of the cells that were divided.	
	Give students a turn to do the same (i.e., put the picture and word cards for cell division in front of the cells that were divided). For students who don't respond, direct them to the model that was divided and say: **This says cell division. This model shows cell division. Cell division is when cells split apart and make more cells.** Read the scientific discovery statement again, pointing to the words on the Student Response Guide page as you read and have the students follow along.	Give praise: **Yes, that's right. You matched the picture of cell division with the cells that divided. These models show how cells divide equally into new cells. That's how living things grow.**

Report

STEP 11		
Materials	**Procedure**	**Follow-up**
• Cell models • Picture and word cards for cell division • KWHL chart • Student Response Guide, pages 96–97: **What did we find out?** and **Why?**	Say: **Let's review what we learned. I asked you what you thought cells do to make living things grow.** Point to the predictions on the KWHL chart. **Some of you said that cells stay together. Some of you said that cells divide. What did we find out? What do cells do to make living things grow? Do they divide or stay together?** Have each student respond orally, use an AAC device to respond, point to a response on the Student Response Guide page, or nod yes or no when you say "divide" or "stay together." Ask students to point to the picture and word cards for cell and then say "cell."	Praise the students and then summarize: **Good, we found out that cells divide to make living things grow.** If any students respond "stay together," point to the models and say: **We learned that cells divide to make more cells. This is how living things grow.** Write "Cells divide" in the open area at the bottom of the KWHL chart.
	Point to the models and ask: **Why do cells divide?** Have each student respond orally, use an AAC device to respond, or point to a response on the Student Response Guide page to indicate that cells divide to make living things grow. Ask students to point to the picture and word cards for cell division and then say "cell division."	Point to the models and say: **Yes, cells divide to make living things grow.** Scaffold for those who don't respond by asking: **Remember, we began the lesson by looking at the models to discover more about living things. What did we want to find out?**

Report

STEP 12		
Materials	**Procedure**	**Follow-up**
• KWHL chart • Student Response Guide, page 98: **What did we learn?**	Say: **Let's review what we learned. Cell division makes living things** _____. Have each student respond orally with "grow," use an AAC device to respond, or point to a response on the Student Response Guide page to fill in the blank.	Point to the models and say: **Yes, living things grow when cells divide. This is called cell division.** Scaffold for those who don't respond by asking: **We saw the model divide. Why do cells divide?** Write "Cell division makes living things grow" in the "Learned (L)" column of the KWHL chart.

Review vocabulary

Materials: Picture and word cards for cell, cell division, bacteria, disease, nutrition

Procedure: Use the time-delay procedure to review each of the vocabulary words for the unit. See page 8 for the procedure.

Extend and review lesson

Read the story on page 34 in **ScienceWork** with the students. Help them apply the scientific concept they learned in this lesson to the story. Complete the exercise following the story together or send it home as homework.

Lesson 4 Bacteria

Concept

Soap destroys bacteria that can cause disease.

Background

In this lesson, students learn that bacteria are living organisms they can't see without the microscope. They learn that they have bacteria and oils on their skin, and the oils allow bacteria to live and grow. Washing with soap and water is important in stopping the spread of bacteria that cause disease.

Materials

- Measuring cup
- Bacteria slide
- Photo of sick person
- 2 clear plastic bowls
- Glitter
- Picture and word cards for cell, cell division, bacteria, disease, nutrition
- KWHL chart
- Safety Rules for Science Class poster
- Student Response Guide, pages 99–109
- ScienceWork, pages 37–40

BRING FROM HOME Cooking or baby oil, hand soap, water, microscope

TO REPLENISH MATERIALS Glitter can be found at any craft store.

Preparation

Using 1 plastic bowl, prepare an oil and glitter mixture by combining about ⅛ cup of oil with 1 teaspoon glitter. Add water to the second plastic bowl for hand washing.

Vocabulary

Review picture and sight word cards for this unit (see pages 82–84).

 **Engage**

STEP 1

Materials	Procedure	Follow-up
<ul><li>Microscope</li><li>Bacteria slide</li><li>Hand soap</li><li>Plastic bowl with glitter-oil mixture</li><li>Plastic bowl with water</li><li>Photo of sick person</li></ul>	Engage the students by telling them: **Today in science we're going to learn more about living things. We're going to learn about bacteria that lives on our skin and hands. Bacteria can make us sick. Let's begin our experiment. Here are some of our materials.**	
	Point to the materials and invite the students to examine them for a few moments, make comments, and ask questions.	If students ask, "What are these?" say: **Good question.**

STEP 2

Materials	Procedure	Follow-up
<ul><li>Microscope</li><li>Bacteria slide</li><li>Hand soap</li><li>Plastic bowl with glitter-oil mixture</li><li>Plastic bowl with water</li><li>Photo of sick person</li><li>Student Response Guide, page 99: **What is this?**</li></ul>	Point to the microscope, the photo, and the soap and ask: **What do you think these are? Make a guess.** Give each student a chance to guess before giving feedback. Remember, you do want students to make guesses in an inquiry lesson. Have each student respond orally with "a microscope," "a sick person," and "soap"; use an AAC device to respond; or point to responses on the Student Response Guide page. Prompt students who don't have symbol use to look at the materials and to touch the pictures in the Student Response Guide. For example, say: **We'll look at a slide under the microscope. You're looking at a microscope.**	Praise correct responses. If students give an incorrect answer, say: **That's a good guess.** Then give a brief reason why the choice isn't the best response. For example, for a window, say: **That's a good guess. It looks like a small window, but it's a microscope.**

 Engage

STEP 3		
Materials	**Procedure**	**Follow-up**
• Microscope • Bacteria slide • Hand soap • Plastic bowl with glitter-oil mixture • Plastic bowl with water • Photo of sick person • KWHL chart • Student Response Guide, page 100: **What do you know?**	Say: **Today we'll learn more about living things and cells. We'll use these materials to learn about bacteria.** Point to the microscope and the hand soap one at a time and ask: **What do you know about this material?** Have the students tell something they know about the materials. Have each student respond orally, use an AAC device to respond, or point to responses on the Student Response Guide page. Prompt students who don't have symbol use to look at the hand soap and to touch the picture of "It's used to wash hands" in the Student Response Guide. For example, say: **Soap is used to wash our hands.**	Praise correct responses. For example, say: **Yes, this is soap. We use soap to wash our hands.** Correct inappropriate answers by giving a brief reason why the response isn't the best response. For example, if "It's used to paint a picture" is chosen, say: **You said this soap is used to paint pictures, but it's used to wash hands.** On the KWHL chart, record the correct answers in the "Know (K)" column.

STEP 4		
Materials	**Procedure**	**Follow-up**
• Microscope • Bacteria slide • Hand soap • Plastic bowl with glitter-oil mixture • Plastic bowl with water • Photo of sick person • KWHL chart • Student Response Guide, page 101: **What do you want to know?**	Point to the soap, the photo, and the bacteria slide and say: **These are all materials we'll use for our experiment. What do you want to know about these materials?** Have students tell anything they might want to know about the materials. Have students respond orally, use their AAC devices to respond, or point to responses on the Student Response Guide page. Prompt students who don't have symbol use to choose any picture response. Provide feedback to students to help build meaning.	Acknowledge any response. For example, if "Will the slide change colors?" is chosen, say: **It would be interesting to find out if the slide changes colors.** Guide students to the answer: "What does soap do to bacteria cells?" Say: **I would like to know what soap does to bacteria cells. How about you?** On the KWHL chart, record this response in the "Want (W)" column.

Investigate and describe relationships

STEP 5

Materials	Procedure	Follow-up
• Microscope • Bacteria slide • Hand soap • Plastic bowl with glitter-oil mixture • Plastic bowl with water • Photo of sick person • KWHL chart • Student Response Guide, page 102: **How can we find out?**	While pointing to the "W" column on the KWHL chart, restate: **We want to know what soap does to bacteria cells.** Then ask: **How can we find out?** Have each student respond orally, use an AAC device to respond, point to a response on the Student Response Guide page, or pantomime washing hands.	If a student gives alternate correct answers or incorrect answers, give a brief demo or explanation. For example, if they answer "Listen to the slide," listen for a moment and say: **Let's listen. I don't hear anything. That didn't give us much information. What else could we do?** After several students respond, acknowledge the one who answers "Do a demonstration with a model," or point to the preferred response and say: **I think the best way to find out what soap does to bacteria is to do a demonstration with a model.** On the KWHL chart, record responses in the "How (H)" column. Circle "Do a demonstration."

Investigate and describe relationships

STEP 6

Materials	Procedure	Follow-up
<ul><li>Microscope</li><li>Bacteria slide</li><li>Hand soap</li><li>Plastic bowl with glitter-oil mixture</li><li>Plastic bowl with water</li><li>Photo of sick person</li><li>KWHL chart</li><li>Safety Rules for Science Class poster</li><li>Student Response Guide, page 103: **What do you think will happen?**</li></ul>	Review the safety rules for science listed on the poster. Point to the bacteria slide and say: **First we'll look at a bacteria cell using the microscope. Bacteria live all around us. They are cells so they are living. Bacteria can cause diseases and make us sick** (show the photo of the sick person). **Bacteria are very tiny so we need to use the microscope to see the bacteria. Then we'll do a demonstration with a model of having bacteria on our hands. We'll find out what happens to bacteria when we use soap on our hands. What do you think soap will do to bacteria? Do you think the soap will make the bacteria grow, or will it destroy the bacteria?**	
	Have each student make a prediction by responding orally, using an AAC device to respond, pointing to a response on the Student Response Guide page, or nodding when you say "make bacteria grow" or "destroy bacteria."	Tally the students' answers—how many said soap makes bacteria grow and how many said soap destroys bacteria—and record them in the open area at the bottom of the KWHL chart to refer to at the end of the lesson.

Investigate and describe relationships

STEP 7

Materials	Procedure	Follow-up
- Microscope - Bacteria slide - Hand soap - Plastic bowl with glitter-oil mixture - Plastic bowl with water	Say: **You just made a prediction. Some of you said the soap will make the bacteria grow, and some of you said the soap will destroy the bacteria. Let's find out.** Point to the bacteria slide and say: **First let's look at the bacteria on this slide under the microscope. It will help us see how small a bacteria cell is. We can't see bacteria with just our eyes, so we don't know if we have it on our skin or not.** Say: **Next we'll use a model of bacteria to show how we can have bacteria on our skin.** Point to the bowl of the glitter-oil mixture. **We'll pretend this glitter is bacteria. Using this model of bacteria, we'll be able to see bacteria with our eyes. I'll put some bacteria on my hand, and then wash my hands in water.** Dip your hand in the glitter-oil mixture and show your hand with glitter on it to the students. Then dip your hand in the bowl of water. Pat your hand dry or let it air dry. You'll still have the glitter-oil mixture on your hand. Then have each student do the same, but use the soap to wash the glitter off.	Describe aloud what you're doing (e.g., **The bacteria on the slide are small, but they live everywhere**). Encourage the students to tell what they see happening (e.g., "Glitter is stuck on your hand"). Be sure students with visual impairments actively participate in the experiment (e.g., by feeling the top of a pin to understand that many bacteria cells can live on that small surface, and feeling the oil and glitter on their hands).

(Step continues)

Investigate and describe relationships

STEP 7—Continued

Materials	Procedure	Follow-up
	Next, (student's name) will get bacteria on his/her hand. But let's see what happens if (student's name) washes his/her hand with water and soap. Let's see if (student's name)'s hand and my hand will look the same. Look to see if the soap made the bacteria grow or removed the bacteria. Dip the student's hand in the glitter-oil mixture and then in the water. Point out that the bacteria (glitter) is still on the student's hand. Put soap on the student's hand, work the soap into the glitter-oil mix on the student's hand, and then rinse in the water. Pat dry or air dry the student's hand. Point out that the bacteria washed away with soap, but it didn't wash away with just water. Repeat for the other students.	

STEP 8

Materials	Procedure	Follow-up
• Microscope • Bacteria slide • Hand soap • Plastic bowl with glitter-oil mixture • Plastic bowl with water • Student Response Guide, page 104: **What's the same?**	Point to your hand with glitter and the students' hands and say: **Think about the experiment and then look at our hands. What's the same about our hands?** Have each student respond orally, use an AAC device to respond, or point to a response on the Student Response Guide page to say all were washed, all had bacteria on them, and all used water. Prompt students who don't have symbol use to look at or touch the water symbol after another student correctly identifies that all used water.	Praise correct responses: Yes, all of our hands had bacteria on them. And all were washed and we all used water to wash them. That makes them the same. If the students are not making a choice or are making an incorrect choice, guide them by saying: We all started with bacteria on our hands, and then we all used water to wash our hands. That makes them the same.

Investigate and describe relationships

	STEP 9	
Materials	**Procedure**	**Follow-up**
• Microscope • Bacteria slide • Hand soap • Plastic bowl with glitter-oil mixture • Plastic bowl with water • Student Response Guide, page 105: **What's different?**	Point to your hand with glitter and the students' hands and say: **Think about the experiment and then look at our hands again. What's different about our hands?** Have each student respond orally, use an AAC device to respond, or point to a response on the Student Response Guide page to say your hand has bacteria on it, and the bacteria is gone from the students' hands. Prompt students who don't have symbol use to look at or touch the symbol for hands after another student correctly identifies that the difference is the bacteria is gone from the students' hands.	Praise correct responses: **Yes, you're right. My hand has bacteria on it, and your hands don't. The bacteria is gone. That makes them different.** If the students are not making a choice or are making an incorrect choice, say: **Look at our hands again.** Hold up your hand and point to a student's hand. **Look at my hand. It's full of bacteria. I didn't wash with soap. Look at your hands. They are clean. The soap destroyed the bacteria.**

Construct explanation

STEP 10

Materials	Procedure	Follow-up
• Picture and word cards for bacteria • Photo of sick person • Student Response Guide, page 106: **What scientific discovery did we make?**	Read the scientific discovery statement once: **Soap destroys bacteria that can cause disease.** Say: **Let's review what we did. We saw in the microscope that bacteria are very small. Small bacteria cells are also on our hands. The skin on our hands makes oils to keep our hands soft. But the oil is also food for the small bacteria cells. Just like we saw with this model** (point to the glitter-oil mixture), **our hands can be covered with bacteria cells. The bacteria can cause disease that makes us sick.** Hold up the photo of a sick person. **The person in this picture is sick because she has a disease or an infection caused by bacteria.** Say: **We need to remove bacteria from our hands. If we remove the oil from our hands, we can destroy the bacteria. We saw that the soap was the best way to remove the oil and the bacteria. We found that soap destroys bacteria that can cause disease.** Then hold up the picture and word cards for bacteria and say: **This is the picture for bacteria, and this word says bacteria. Say "bacteria."** Put the picture and word cards for bacteria in front of the glitter-oil mixture.	

(Step continues)

Construct explanation

Materials	Procedure	Follow-up
	Give students a turn to do the same (i.e., put the picture and word cards for bacteria in front of glitter-oil mixture). For students who don't respond, show them the photo of a sick person and say: **This person is sick from bacteria.** Point to the picture of bacteria. Read the scientific discovery statement again, pointing to the words on the Student Response Guide page as you read and have the students follow along.	Give praise: **Yes, soap removes bacteria. Say "bacteria."**

Report

STEP 11		
Materials	**Procedure**	**Follow-up**
<ul><li>Picture and word cards for bacteria</li><li>KWHL chart</li><li>Student Response Guide, pages 107–108: **What did we find out?** and **Why?**</li></ul>	Say: **Let's review what we learned. I asked you what you thought the soap would do to bacteria.** Point to the predictions on the KWHL chart. **Some of you said that soap will make the bacteria grow. Some of you said soap will destroy the bacteria. What did we find out? What did the soap do to the bacteria—make it grow or destroy it?** Have each student respond orally, use an AAC device to respond, point to a response on the Student Response Guide page, or nod yes or no when you say "made it grow" or "destroyed the bacteria." Ask students to point to the picture and word cards for bacteria and then say "bacteria."	Praise the students and then summarize: **Good, you said that soap helped remove bacteria from your hands. Soap destroyed the bacteria. The water without soap didn't remove the bacteria on my hands.** If any students respond "made the bacteria grow," say: **We both had bacteria on our hands before we washed. When I washed with water alone, the bacteria did not come off. When all of you washed with soap and water, most of the bacteria came off. The soap helped destroy the bacteria.** Write "Soap helps destroy bacteria" in the open area at the bottom of the KWHL chart.
	Point to the soap and ask: **Why did the soap destroy the bacteria?** Have each student respond orally, use an AAC device to respond, or point to a response on the Student Response Guide page to indicate that the soap removed the oil that the bacteria needed to live. Ask students to point to the picture and word cards for bacteria and then say "bacteria."	Point to the soap and say: **Yes, we saw that the soap removed the oil bacteria need to live.** Scaffold for those who don't respond by saying: **Remember, our skin has oil on it that bacteria need to live. Soap removes the oil and destroys the bacteria.**

Report

STEP 12		
Materials	**Procedure**	**Follow-up**
• KWHL chart • Student Response Guide, page 109: **What did we learn?**	Say: **Let's review what we learned. We learned that soap helps destroy bacteria that can cause _____.** Have each student respond orally with "disease," use an AAC device to respond, or point to a response on the Student Response Guide page to fill in the blank.	Praise the correct response: **That's right. The soap destroys bacteria that can cause disease. Disease makes us sick, and none of us wants to be sick.** Scaffold for those who respond with "nutrition" by saying: **Remember that bacteria must have oil from our skin to live and grow. Soap removes the oil and destroys the bacteria.** Write "Soap helps destroy bacteria that can cause disease" in the "Learned (L)" column of the KWHL chart.

Review vocabulary

Materials: Picture and word cards for cell, cell division, bacteria, disease, nutrition

Procedure: Use the time-delay procedure to review each of the vocabulary words for the unit. See page 8 for the procedure.

Extend and review lesson

Read the story on pages 37–38 in **ScienceWork** with the students. Help them apply the scientific concept they learned in this lesson to the story. Complete the exercise following the story together or send it home as homework.

Lesson 5 Nutrition

Concept

Good nutrition builds healthy cells.

Background

In this lesson, students learn how nutrition affects their cells. They learn that good nutrition builds healthy cells. They study the food pyramid as a way to know that a balance of food from each food group keeps their bodies the healthiest.

Materials

- Picture and word cards for cell, cell division, bacteria, disease, nutrition
- Food pictures, pages 95 and 97 in the ScienceWork pdf on the CD-ROM
- KWHL chart
- Safety Rules for Science Class poster
- Student Response Guide, pages 110–120
- ScienceWork, pages 41–44 and 89–97

BRING FROM HOME

3 paper plates

TO REPLENISH MATERIALS

You'll find more information about the My Food Pyramid at www.mypyramid.gov. You can also print more pyramids from this government website.

Preparation

Prepare for the lesson by selecting, printing, and cutting apart the food pictures from the ScienceWork pdf. Number the plates 1, 2, and 3. Gently attach (food will be removed later in the lesson so a small piece of tape is all that's needed) the food to the paper plates in this way:

Plate 1: fruits and vegetables
Plate 2: vegetables only
Plate 3: food from all food groups

Vocabulary

Review picture and sight word cards for this unit (see pages 82–84).

 **Engage**

STEP 1		
Materials	**Procedure**	**Follow-up**
3 plates with food	Engage the students by telling them: **Today in science we're going to learn more about cells. We'll learn that we can keep our cells healthy by eating well. Another word for food is nutrition. Let's begin our experiment. Here are some of our materials.**	
	Point to the 3 plates with food. Invite the students to examine them for a few moments, make comments, and ask questions.	If students ask, "What are these?" say: **Good question.**

STEP 2		
Materials	**Procedure**	**Follow-up**
• 3 plates with food • Student Response Guide, page 110: **What is this?**	Point to the food on the plates and ask: **What do you think these are? Make a guess.** Give each student a chance to guess before giving feedback. Remember, you do want students to make guesses in an inquiry lesson. Have each student respond orally with "food," use an AAC device to respond, or point to responses on the Student Response Guide page. Prompt students who don't have symbol use to look at the food and to touch the picture of food in the Student Response Guide. For example, say: **You're looking at pictures of food. Touch the food.**	Praise correct responses. If students give an incorrect answer, say: **That's a good guess.** Then give a brief reason why the choice isn't the best response. For example, for "lava," say: **That's a good guess, but that's not lava. You're looking at different types of food.**

Engage

	STEP 3	
Materials	**Procedure**	**Follow-up**
• 3 plates with food • KWHL chart • Student Response Guide, page 111: **What do you know?**	Point to the plates of food and say: **Today we'll learn more about foods and how good nutrition and good food keep our cells healthy.** Then ask: **What do you know about the foods on the plates?** Have the students tell something they know about the different foods. Have each student respond orally, use an AAC device to respond, or point to responses on the Student Response Guide page. Prompt students who don't have symbol use to look at the food and to touch the picture showing food in the Student Response Guide. For example, say: **You're looking at food. We eat food to be healthy.**	Praise correct responses. Point to the food and say: **Yes, these plates have different food on them, and food tastes good.** Correct inappropriate answers by giving a brief reason why the response isn't the best response. For example, if "They dance" is chosen, say: **I don't think the food dances. We can eat the food.** On the KWHL chart, record the correct answers in the "Know (K)" column.

Engage

STEP 4		
Materials	**Procedure**	**Follow-up**
• 3 plates with food • ScienceWork, pages 89–90: **Nutrition chart** • KWHL chart • Student Response Guide, page 112: **What do you want to know?**	Review the **Nutrition chart** with the students. Say: This picture shows us that the food we eat helps certain parts of our bodies. The body is made of cells. Different foods, like the foods on these plates, help us keep our cells healthy. This chart tells us what each vitamin does for our bodies. It also tells us which foods give us which vitamins. Continue to read what different vitamins and foods do for our bodies on the chart. Then point to the food on the plates and ask: What do you want to know about the food on these plates? Have students tell anything they might want to know about the food. Have students respond orally, use their AAC devices to respond, or point to responses on the Student Response Guide page. Prompt students who don't have symbol use to choose any picture response. Provide feedback to students to help build meaning.	Acknowledge any response. For example, if "Can food sing?" is chosen, say: I don't hear any singing. What else could we find out? Guide students to the answer: "Which plate of food can help us stay healthy?" Say: I would like to know which plate of food can help us stay healthy. On the KWHL chart, record this response in the "Want (W)" column.

Investigate and describe relationships

STEP 5

Materials	Procedure	Follow-up
<ul><li>3 plates with food</li><li>ScienceWork, pages 89–90: **Nutrition chart**</li><li>KWHL chart</li><li>Student Response Guide, page 113: **How can we find out?**</li></ul>	While pointing to the "W" column on the KWHL chart, restate: We want to know which plate of food can help us stay healthy. Then ask: How can we find out? Have each student respond orally, use an AAC device to respond, point to a response on the Student Response Guide page, or pantomime what to do.	If students give alternate correct answers or incorrect answers, give a brief demo or explanation. For example, if they answer "Weigh the food," say: Weighing the food would be interesting, but it doesn't tell us which foods can help us stay healthy. What else could we do? After several students respond, acknowledge the one who answers "Compare the food on the plates" or point to the preferred response and say: I think the easiest way to know which plate of food can help us stay healthy is to compare the food on the plates. On the KWHL chart, record responses in the "How (H)" column. Circle "Compare the food on the plates."

Investigate and describe relationships

STEP 6

Materials	Procedure	Follow-up
<ul><li>3 plates with food</li><li>ScienceWork, pages 89–90: **Nutrition chart**</li><li>ScienceWork, page 91: **My food pyramid**</li><li>KWHL chart</li><li>Safety Rules for Science Class poster</li><li>Student Response Guide, page 114: **What do you think will happen?**</li></ul>	Review the safety rules for science listed on the poster. Refer students to the **My food pyramid**.* Say: **This is a food pyramid. These are food groups on the pyramid. Each food group on the pyramid tells how much food in that group you should eat. The body running up the steps tells you that you also need to have physical exercise to be healthy. We'll talk more about the food groups today.** Continue the discussion of the **My food pyramid*** if you desire. Point to food on the plates and say: **We're going to compare the food on each plate to the food pyramid. You'll decide which food fits into the different groups. Then we'll look at how much of each food item is healthy for us to eat. Then you can decide which plate has the healthiest food. Which plate of food do you think will help us stay healthy—plate 1, plate 2, or plate 3?**	
	Have each student make a prediction by responding orally, using an AAC device to respond, pointing to a plate or a response on the Student Response Guide page, or nodding when you say "plate 1," "plate 2," or "plate 3."	Tally the students' answers—how many said plate 1, plate 2, or plate 3—and record them in the open area at the bottom of the KWHL chart to refer to at the end of the lesson.

***My food pyramid** contains 8 divisions. From left to right on the pyramid are 6 food groups:

- Grains, recommending that at least half of grains consumed be as whole grains
- Vegetables, emphasizing dark green vegetables, orange vegetables, and dry beans and peas
- Fruits, emphasizing variety and deemphasizing fruit juices
- Oils, recommending fish, nut, and vegetable sources
- Milk, a category that includes other dairy products
- Meat and beans, emphasizing low-fat and lean meats such as fish as well as more beans, peas, nuts, and seeds

There are two other categories:

- Physical activity, represented by a person climbing steps on the pyramid, with at least 30 minutes of moderate to vigorous activity per day recommended (and in some cases 60 or 90 minutes)
- Discretionary calories, represented by the uncolored tip of the pyramid, including items such as candy, alcohol, or additional food from any other group

Investigate and describe relationships

STEP 7

Materials	Procedure	Follow-up
• 3 plates with sorted food • ScienceWork, pages 89–90: **Nutrition chart** • ScienceWork, page 91: **My food pyramid** • ScienceWork, pages 92–93: blank **My food pyramid** (It might be helpful to print pyramids from the ScienceWork pdf.)	Say: **You just made a prediction. Some of you said the food on plate 1 will help us stay healthy, some said plate 2, and some said plate 3. Let's find out.** Point out the different food groups again on the food pyramid and discuss what types of food go in each group (e.g., bananas in the fruit group, broccoli in the vegetable group, bread in the grain group). Say: **It's important to eat foods from all of the different categories. Let's move food off of the plates and onto the food pyramid. Let's put them in the group they belong in.** Have one or two students work together to remove food from plate 1 and move it to the blank **My food pyramid** in their ScienceWork books.* Have one or two students work together to remove food from plate 2 and move it to a blank **My food pyramid.** Finally, have one or two students work together to remove food from plate 3 and move it to a blank **My food pyramid.**	Describe aloud what you're doing. Encourage the students to tell what they're doing (e.g., "Bread goes in grains"). Praise them for putting foods in the correct groups. Be sure students with visual impairments actively participate in the experiment (e.g., hand the student an item and name it; ask which group the food should go in or give two choices). If students put items in the wrong groups, redirect them (e.g., **Let's look again. This apple is fruit. It goes in the fruit and vegetable group**).

*Each student's ScienceWork includes a blank **My food pyramid** and pictures of food for sorting. Sorting food on the pyramid is a great extension activity to send home with the students.

Investigate and describe relationships

STEP 8

Materials	Procedure	Follow-up
• 3 food pyramids with food sorted on them • Student Response Guide, page 115: **What's the same?**	Point to the food pyramids with the food sorted on them and say: **Here are the food pyramids where you sorted the food. What's the same about the food pyramids?** Have each student respond orally, use an AAC device to respond, or point to a response on the Student Response Guide page to say there's food on the pyramids. Prompt students who don't have symbol use to look at or touch the food after another student correctly identifies that there's food on the pyramids.	Praise correct responses: **Yes, there's food on all of the pyramids. That makes them the same.** If the students are not making a choice or are making an incorrect choice, guide them by saying: **Look at the 3 pyramids we sorted the food onto. All of the pyramids have food on them. That makes them the same.**

STEP 9

Materials	Procedure	Follow-up
• 3 food pyramids with food sorted on them • Student Response Guide, page 116: **What's different?**	Point to the food pyramids with the food sorted on them and say: **Now look at the food pyramids again. You sorted the food into the different categories on the pyramids. What's different about the pyramids?** Have each student respond orally, use an AAC device to respond, or point to a response on the Student Response Guide page to say the pyramids have different types of food and different amounts of food. Prompt students who don't have symbol use to look at or touch the food after another student correctly identifies that the difference is the type and amount of food.	Praise correct responses: **Yes, the type of food and the amount of food in the categories is different. The first pyramid has food only in the fruit and vegetable categories. The second pyramid has food only in the vegetable category. But the third pyramid has food in all the categories. That makes them different.** If the students are not making a choice or are making an incorrect choice, guide them by saying: **Remember, we sorted the food into different categories on the food pyramid. Only one of the pyramids** (point to the pyramid with food from plate 3) **has food in all of the categories. That makes the pyramids different.**

Construct explanation

STEP 10		
Materials	**Procedure**	**Follow-up**
• 3 food pyramids with food sorted on them • Picture and word cards for nutrition • ScienceWork, pages 89–90: **Nutrition chart** • Student Response Guide, page 117: **What scientific discovery did we make?**	Read the scientific discovery statement once: **To stay healthy, we need good nutrition. Good nutrition builds healthy cells.** Say: **Let's review what we did. First we looked at this Nutrition chart** (point to the **Nutrition chart**) **that shows us how different foods help different parts of our bodies. What we eat helps us stay healthy. To stay healthy we need good nutrition.** **Then we sorted plates of food into different categories on a food pyramid. One of the plates had food in all of the different categories. When you eat different types of healthy food, you're keeping your body healthy with good nutrition. Good nutrition builds healthy cells.** Put the picture and word cards for nutrition in front of the last food pyramid and say: **This is the picture for nutrition, and this word says nutrition. Say "nutrition."**	
	Give students a turn to do the same (i.e., put the picture and word cards for nutrition in front of the food pyramid). For students who don't respond, direct them to look at the correct pyramid while you or a peer places the picture and word cards. Read the scientific discovery statement again, pointing to the words on the Student Response Guide page as you read and have the students follow along.	Give praise: **Yes, if we eat foods similar to the food on this pyramid, our bodies will get the good nutrition bodies need.**

Report

STEP 11		
Materials	**Procedure**	**Follow-up**
• 3 food pyramids with food sorted on them • Picture and word cards for nutrition • KWHL chart • Student Response Guide, pages 118–119: **What did we find out?** and **Why?**	Say: **Let's review what we learned. When we sorted the food onto the pyramids, we discovered that different foods belong in different food groups. It's important to eat food from different food groups so we stay healthy. To stay healthy we need good nutrition. Good nutrition builds healthy cells.** Point to the predictions on the KWHL chart. **I asked you which plate of food you thought would help us stay healthy. Then we sorted the food onto the pyramids. Some of you thought it would be the food on plate 1. Some of you thought it would be the food on plate 2. Some of you thought it would be the food on plate 3. Which plate of food will help us stay the healthiest?** Have each student respond orally, use an AAC device to respond, point to a response on the Student Response Guide page, or nod yes or no when you say "plate 1," "plate 2," or "plate 3." Ask students to point to the picture and word cards for nutrition and then say "nutrition."	Praise the students and then summarize: **Good, we learned that to stay healthy we need to eat food from all of the different food groups. Plate 3 had food from all categories. Plate 3 would give us good nutrition and help us stay the healthiest.** If any students respond "plate 1" or "plate 2," point to the pyramid with food from plate 3 and say: **We learned that we need food from all food groups.** Write "Good nutrition builds healthy cells" in the open area at the bottom of the KWHL chart.
	Point to a food pyramid and ask: **Why is it important to have good nutrition?** Have each student respond orally, use an AAC device to respond, or point to a response on the Student Response Guide page to indicate that good nutrition builds healthy cells. Ask students to point to the picture and word cards for nutrition and then say "nutrition."	Point to a food pyramid and say: **Yes, good nutrition builds healthy cells.** Scaffold for those who don't respond by saying: **It's important to take care of our bodies to help us grow. Remember that our bodies are made of cells and we need to keep the cells healthy.**

Report

STEP 12		
Materials	**Procedure**	**Follow-up**
• 3 food pyramids with food sorted on them • KWHL chart • Student Response Guide, page 120: **What did we learn?**	Say: **Let's review what we learned. To stay healthy, we need good** _____. Have each student respond orally with "nutrition," use an AAC device to respond, or point to a response on the Student Response Guide page to fill in the blank.	Point to a food pyramid and say: **Yes, we looked at the food pyramid and found out that we need to eat food in different groups to stay healthy.** Scaffold for those who don't respond by asking: **When we eat food from all food groups, what are we getting? We get good** _____. Write "To stay healthy, we need good nutrition" in the "Learned (L)" column of the KWHL chart.

Review vocabulary

Materials: Picture and word cards for cell, cell division, bacteria, disease, nutrition

Procedure: Use the time-delay procedure to review each of the vocabulary words for the unit. See page 8 for the procedure.

Extend and review lesson

Read the story on pages 41–42 in **ScienceWork** with the students. Help them apply the scientific concept they learned in this lesson to the story. Complete the exercise following the story together or send it home as homework.

Unit C Waters

Lesson 1 Precipitation

Concept

When water droplets in clouds get heavy, the water falls out as precipitation.

Background

In this lesson, students begin to learn about the Earth's water cycle. They learn that clouds create precipitation when the water droplets in the clouds get heavy. They learn that there are several forms of precipitation. This lesson uses a model to demonstrate the concept of precipitation. Sponges are used as models of clouds.

Materials

- 2 clear plastic bowls
- 2 clear plastic cups
- 2 sponges
- Picture and word card for precipitation, evaporation, condensation, pollution, conservation
- Photo of clouds
- KWHL chart
- Safety Rules for Science Class poster
- Student Response Guide, pages 122–132
- ScienceWork, pages 46–48

 Water

Preparation

Prepare for this lesson by filling one of the cups full of water and the other cup with a small amount of water.

Vocabulary

Teach picture symbols and sight words for this unit (see pages 138–140) to familiarize students with the vocabulary introduced in this lesson.

Engage

STEP 1		
Materials	**Procedure**	**Follow-up**
2 cups with water	Engage the students by telling them: **Today in science we're going to learn about precipitation and the Earth's water cycle. Let's begin our experiment. Here are some of our materials.** Point to the two cups with water. Invite the students to examine them for a few moments, make comments, and ask questions.	If students ask, "What are these?" say: **Good question.**

STEP 2		
Materials	**Procedure**	**Follow-up**
• 2 cups with water • Picture and word cards for precipitation • Student Response Guide, page 122: **What is this?**	Point to the water in one of the cups and ask: **What do you think this is? Make a guess.** Give each student a chance to guess before giving feedback. Remember, you do want students to make guesses in an inquiry lesson. Have each student respond orally with "liquid," "water," "rain," or "precipitation"; use an AAC device to respond; or point to responses on the Student Response Guide page. Prompt students who don't have symbol use to look at the water in a cup and touch the picture of the water in the Student Response Guide. For example, say: **You're looking at water. This is water.** After the students have guessed, guide them to point to precipitation in the Student Response Guide. Explain to students that rain, snow, and ice are all types of precipitation. Hold up the picture and word cards for precipitation and say: **This is the picture of precipitation, and this word says precipitation. Say "precipitation."**	Praise correct responses. If students give an incorrect answer, say: **That's a good guess.** Then give a brief reason why the choice isn't the best response. For example, for "juice," say: **It looks a little bit like juice, but it's actually water.**

 **Engage**

STEP 3

Materials	Procedure	Follow-up
• 2 cups with water • KWHL chart • Student Response Guide, page 123: **What do you know?**	Point to one of the cups with water and say: **What do you know about the material in this cup?** Have the students tell something they know about the water. Have each student respond orally, use an AAC device to respond, or point to responses on the Student Response Guide page. Prompt students who don't have symbol use to look at the cup of water and to touch the picture of "It's wet" in the Student Response Guide. For example, say: **You're looking at the water. The water is wet.**	Praise correct responses. Correct inappropriate answers by giving a brief reason why the response isn't the best response. For example, if "It's dry" is chosen, say: **I don't think the water is dry. Feel the water. See, the water is wet.** On the KWHL chart, record the correct answers in the "Know (K)" column.

STEP 4

Materials	Procedure	Follow-up
• 2 cups with water • 2 sponges • Photo of clouds • KWHL chart • Student Response Guide, page 124: **What do you want to know?**	Introduce the sponge and review the concept of using a model in science. Say: **This is a sponge. Today in science the sponge will be a model of a cloud.** Then show the students the picture of the clouds. Ask them to touch the cloud model (the sponge). Place the picture of the clouds next to the sponge. **What do you want to know about the clouds and the water?** Have students tell anything they might want to know about the clouds and the water. Have students respond orally, use their AAC devices to respond, or point to responses on the Student Response Guide page. Prompt students who don't have symbol use to choose any picture response. Provide feedback to students to help build meaning.	Acknowledge any response. For example, if "Will the clouds change colors?" is chosen, say: **It would be interesting to find out if the clouds change colors.** Guide students to the answer: "What will happen if we pour water into the clouds?" Say: **I would like to know what will happen if we pour water into the clouds. How about you?** On the KWHL chart, record this response in the "Want (W)" column.

Investigate and describe relationships

STEP 5

Materials	Procedure	Follow-up
• 2 cups with water • 2 sponges • Photo of clouds • KWHL chart • Student Response Guide, page 125: **How can we find out?**	While pointing to the "W" column on the KWHL chart, restate: **We want to know what will happen if we pour water into these clouds.** Then ask: **How can we find out?** Have each student respond orally, use an AAC device to respond, point to a response on the Student Response Guide page, or pantomime pouring the water into the sponge.	If students give alternate correct answers or incorrect answers, give a brief demo or explanation. For example, if they answer "Touch them," let them touch the sponges and say: **That didn't give us much information. What else could we do?** After several students respond, acknowledge the one who answers "Add water to them," or point to the preferred response and say: **I think the easiest way to find out what will happen is to add water to these clouds.** On the KWHL chart, record responses in the "How (H)" column. Circle "Add water to them."

STEP 6

Materials	Procedure	Follow-up
• 2 cups with water • 2 sponges • Photo of clouds • KWHL chart • Safety Rules for Science Class poster • Student Response Guide, page 126: **What do you think will happen?**	Review the safety rules for science listed on the poster. Point to the sponges and say: **We'll pour the water from this cup into this cloud. We'll pour the little bit of water from this cup into this cloud. Precipitation occurs when water falls out of the clouds. Do you think both clouds will create precipitation? Remember, the water is precipitation in this model. Do you think both clouds will create precipitation—yes or no?**	
	Have each student make a prediction by responding orally, using an AAC device to respond, pointing to a response on the Student Response Guide page, or nodding.	Tally the students' answers—how many said yes and how many said no—and record them in the open area at the bottom of the KWHL chart to refer to at the end of the lesson.

Investigate and describe relationships

Materials	Procedure	Follow-up
• 2 cups with water • 2 sponges • 2 clear plastic bowls	Say: **You just made a prediction. Some of you said both clouds will create precipitation, and some of you said they won't. Let's find out.** Hold a sponge over one of the clear plastic bowls. Have a student pour the cup with the small amount of water into the "cloud." Squeeze the sponge slightly. Say: **This cloud has no water droplets. It has no rain. Even though we put a little bit of water in this cloud, the water droplets were not heavy enough to come out as rain.** Hold the second sponge over the other clear bowl. Have one student pour the full cup of water into the "cloud." Squeeze the sponge slightly. Say: **Look, this cloud created rain. The water droplets in this cloud got so heavy that they soaked through the cloud. The water droplets came out of the cloud as rain.** While holding up the picture of the clouds, say: **Here's what a cloud looks like. This cloud has water droplets in it, and when the water droplets get too heavy, they fall out of the clouds as precipitation.**	Describe aloud what the students are seeing (e.g., **Look at the water dripping out of this cloud**). Encourage the students to tell what they see (e.g., "It's raining"). Be sure students with visual impairments actively participate in the experiment (e.g., by placing their hands under the clouds to feel the rain or the absence of rain).

Investigate and describe relationships

STEP 8

Materials	Procedure	Follow-up
• 2 sponges • 2 clear plastic bowls • Student Response Guide, page 127: **What's the same?**	Point to the clouds (sponges) and say: **Here are our models of clouds. What's the same about both of these models?** Have each student respond orally, use an AAC device to respond, or point to a response on the Student Response Guide page to say both are wet and both are clouds. Prompt students who don't have symbol use to look at or touch the clouds after another student correctly identifies that both are clouds.	Praise correct responses: **Yes, both are wet, and both are clouds. We added water to both, and that made them wet. That makes them the same.** If the students are not making a choice or are making an incorrect choice, guide the students by saying: **Feel both of the clouds. How do they feel? Here's the cup that we poured water from. Remember, the water made the clouds wet** (pretend to pour the water into the clouds again). **They both feel wet from the water. That makes them the same.**

STEP 9

Materials	Procedure	Follow-up
• 2 sponges • 2 clear plastic bowls • Photo of clouds • Student Response Guide, page 128: **What's different?**	Point to the clouds (sponges) again and say: **Here are our models of clouds. We put a small amount of water in one, and we put a full cup of water in the other. What is different about the cloud models?** Have each student respond orally, use an AAC device to respond, or point to a response on the Student Response Guide page to say one showed precipitation. Prompt students who don't have symbol use to look at or touch the cloud that created precipitation after another student correctly identifies that one showed precipitation. Point to the photo of clouds. **Clouds hold water until the water droplets get heavy. Then the water falls out as precipitation.**	Praise correct responses: **Yes, one produced precipitation. That cloud was heavier with water, so it created precipitation. The other cloud did not. That makes them different.** If the students are not making a choice or are making an incorrect choice, say: **How much water did we add to the clouds? Was it the same amount?** Point to the cloud models. **No, they had different amounts of water in them.**

Construct explanation

STEP 10

Materials	Procedure	Follow-up
<ul><li>2 sponges</li><li>2 clear plastic bowls</li><li>Picture and word cards for precipitation</li><li>Photo of clouds</li><li>Student Response Guide, page 129: **What scientific discovery did we make?**</li></ul>	Read the scientific discovery statement once: **When water droplets in clouds get heavy, the water falls out as precipitation.** Say: **Let's review what we did. First we poured a little bit of water into this cloud.** (Touch the sponge with the small amount of water.) **Then we added a lot of water to this cloud.** (Touch sponge with the larger amount of water.) **The cloud got heavy with water droplets. When the water droplets got too heavy, the water fell out of the cloud as precipitation.** Then hold up the picture and word cards for precipitation and say: **This is the picture for precipitation, and this word says precipitation. Say "precipitation."** Put the sight word and picture card for precipitation in front of the cloud model.	
	Give students a turn to do the same (i.e., put the picture and word cards in front of the cloud models). For students who don't respond, have them put the picture card in front of a cloud model and then guide them to match the word card. Other students may be prompted to look at the model of the cloud while you or a peer places the picture and word cards. Read the scientific discovery statement again, pointing to the words on the Student Response Guide page as you read and having the students follow along.	Give praise: **Yes, this is precipitation. Precipitation fell out of this cloud. Say "precipitation."**

Report

STEP 11

Materials	Procedure	Follow-up
• 2 sponges • Picture and word cards for precipitation • Photo of clouds • KWHL chart • Student Response Guide, pages 130–131: **What did we find out?** and **Why?**	Say: **Let's review what we learned. I asked if you thought both clouds would create precipitation.** Point to the predictions on the KWHL chart. **Some of you said yes, and some of you said no. Did both clouds create precipitation—yes or no?** Have each student respond orally, use an AAC device to respond, point to a response on the Student Response Guide page, or nod yes or no.	Praise the students and then summarize: **Good, what happened was that this cloud was full of water. The cloud was heavy with water so it created precipitation. The other cloud did not. Only one cloud created precipitation.** If any students respond "yes," show a model of a cloud and say: **Did this cloud make rain?** Write "No—one cloud created precipitation" in the open area at the bottom of the KWHL chart.
	Point to the cloud model and ask: **Why did one cloud create precipitation?** Have each student respond orally, use an AAC device to respond, or point to a response on the Student Response Guide page to indicate it got heavy with water. Ask students to point to the picture and word cards for precipitation and then say "precipitation."	Point to the cloud model and say: **Yes, the one cloud was full of water. The water got heavy, and it created rain. Rain is a type of precipitation.** Scaffold for those who don't respond by saying: **When you added a lot of water to the cloud, the cloud got what?**

STEP 12

Materials	Procedure	Follow-up
• KWHL chart • Student Response Guide, page 132 **What did we learn?**	Say: **Let's review what we learned. When water droplets in clouds get heavy, they** _____. Have each student respond orally with "become precipitation," use an AAC device to respond, or point to a response on the Student Response Guide page to fill in the blank.	Say: **Yes, they become precipitation.** Scaffold for students who say "turn into thunder" or "make music" by pointing to the cloud model and saying: **Both clouds were wet, but only one got heavy. What happens if water in the clouds gets heavy?** Write "When water droplets in clouds get heavy, the water falls out as precipitation" in the "Learned (L)" column of the KWHL chart.

Teach vocabulary

Materials	Procedure	Follow-up
Picture cards: • precipitation • evaporation • condensation • pollution • conservation	Review the picture cards with students individually when possible. In this first round, give the student a prompt without delay (zero time delay). Place the picture cards in front of the student. Say: **Show me (precipitation)** and point to the card as you ask the student to point (zero time delay). Shuffle the cards. Repeat this procedure for the remaining 4 cards.	If the student points correctly, give praise: **Good! You pointed to (precipitation). Say (precipitation).** If the student doesn't point, provide physical guidance to point.
	In this second round of vocabulary review, give the student up to 5 seconds to respond independently (5-second time delay). Shuffle the picture cards, place them in front of the student, and say: **Point to (precipitation).** Repeat this process for the remaining 4 cards.	If the student points correctly, give praise: **Good! You pointed to (precipitation) by yourself. Say (precipitation).** If the student doesn't point, model pointing and say: **This is (precipitation). Point to (precipitation). Say (precipitation).** If the student makes an error, point to the correct answer and say: **This is (precipitation). Point to (precipitation). Say (precipitation).** Shuffle the cards and repeat this process for the remaining 4 cards.

Teach vocabulary

Materials	Procedure	Follow-up
Word cards: • precipitation • evaporation • condensation • pollution • conservation	Review the word cards with students individually if possible. In this first round, give the student a prompt without delay (zero time delay). Place the word cards in front of the student. Say: **Show me (precipitation)** and point to the card as you ask the student to point (zero time delay). Shuffle the cards. Repeat this procedure for the remaining 4 cards.	If the student points correctly, give praise: **Good! You pointed to (precipitation). Say (precipitation).** If the student doesn't point, provide physical guidance to point.
	In this second round of vocabulary review, give the student up to 5 seconds to respond independently (5-second time delay). Shuffle the word cards, place them in front of the student, and say: **Point to (precipitation).** Repeat this process for the remaining 4 cards.	If the student points correctly, give praise: **Good! You pointed to (precipitation) by yourself. Say (precipitation).** If the student doesn't point, model pointing and say: **This is (precipitation). Point to (precipitation). Say (precipitation).** If the student makes an error, point to the correct answer and say: **This is (precipitation). Point to (precipitation). Say (precipitation).** Shuffle the cards and repeat this process for the remaining 4 cards.

Teach vocabulary

Materials	Procedure	Follow-up
Picture and word cards: • precipitation • evaporation • condensation • pollution • conservation	In the first round, place the word cards in front of the student. Then hand a picture card to the student and say: **Match this picture to the word.** Match the picture card to the word card as you ask the student to match them (zero time delay). Shuffle the cards. Repeat this procedure for the remaining 4 cards.	If the student matches correctly, give praise: **Good! You matched the picture to the word. Say (precipitation).** If the student doesn't match the cards, provide physical guidance to point.
	In a second round, give the student up to 5 seconds to match 2 cards independently (5-second time delay). Repeat this process for the remaining 4 cards.	If the student matches correctly, give praise: **Good! You matched the two cards by yourself. Say (precipitation).** If the student doesn't match the cards, model matching and say: **This is (precipitation). Match this card to the word (precipitation). Say (precipitation).** If the student makes an error, point to the correct answer and say: **This is (precipitation). Match this card to (precipitation). Say (precipitation).** Shuffle the cards and repeat this process for the remaining 4 cards.

Reviewing vocabulary in a group

If reviewing vocabulary in a group, follow the format described, but have one student respond while you cue the others to watch. Pick a second student at random to repeat the response from time to time to be sure everyone is watching.

Extend and review lesson

Read the story on pages 46–47 in **ScienceWork** with the students. Help them apply the scientific concept they learned in this lesson to the story. Complete the exercise following the story together or send it home as homework.

Lesson 2 Evaporation

Concept

When water is heated, it turns into steam. This is called evaporation.

Background

In this lesson, students learn more about the Earth's water cycle. They learn about the effect of temperature on water by observing water evaporate to steam when it's heated.

Materials

- 2 measuring cups
- Picture and word card for precipitation, evaporation, condensation, pollution, conservation
- Heated/Not Heated table mat (TM.pdf from the CD-ROM)
- KWHL chart
- Safety Rules for Science Class poster
- Student Response Guide, pages 133–143
- ScienceWork, pages 49–51

BRING FROM HOME Heat source (e.g., microwave, hot plate, electric pan, electric tea kettle), water

Preparation

Prepare for this lesson by printing the Heated/Not Heated table mat from the CD-ROM and filling the 2 measuring cups with water.

Vocabulary

Review picture and sight word cards for this unit (see pages 138–140).

Engage

STEP 1

Materials	Procedure	Follow-up
• 2 measuring cups with water • Heat source	Engage the students by telling them: **Today in science we're going to learn more about the Earth's water cycle. We're going to learn about evaporation. Let's begin our experiment. Here are some of our materials.**	
	Point to the 2 cups with water and the heat source. Invite the students to examine them for a few moments, make comments, and ask questions.	If students ask, "What are these?" say: **Good question.**

STEP 2

Materials	Procedure	Follow-up
• 2 measuring cups with water • Heat source • Picture and word cards for evaporation • Student Response Guide, page 133: **What is this?**	Point to the two measuring cups and the heating source and ask: **What do you think these are? Make a guess.** Give each student a chance to guess before giving feedback. Remember, you do want students to make guesses in an inquiry lesson. Have each student respond orally with "measuring cup," "heater," and "water"; use an AAC device to respond; or point to responses on the Student Response Guide page. Prompt students who don't have symbol use to look at the water in a cup and touch the picture of the water in the Student Response Guide. For example, say: **You're looking at water. This is water.**	Praise correct responses. If students give an incorrect answer, say: **That's a good guess.** Then give a brief reason why the choice isn't the best response. For example, for "milk," say: **It looks a little bit like milk, but it's actually water.**

 **Engage**

STEP 3

Materials	Procedure	Follow-up
• 2 measuring cups with water • Heat source • KWHL chart • Student Response Guide, page 134: **What do you know?**	Point to one of the cups with water and say: **What do you know about material in this cup?** Have the students tell something they know about the water. Have each student respond orally, use an AAC device to respond, or point to responses on the Student Response Guide page. Prompt students who don't have symbol use to look at the cup of water and to touch the picture of "It's wet" in the Student Response Guide. For example, say: **You're looking at the water. The water is wet.**	Praise correct responses. Correct inappropriate answers by giving a brief reason why the response isn't the best response. For example, if "It's dry" is chosen, say: **I don't think the water is dry. Feel the water. See, the water is wet.** On the KWHL chart, record the correct answers in the "Know (K)" column.

STEP 4

Materials	Procedure	Follow-up
• 2 measuring cups with water • Heat source • KWHL chart • Student Response Guide, page 135: **What do you want to know?**	Point to the heat source. Say: **This is something we'll use to heat things. We'll use it to heat the water. We'll need to be very careful in this experiment because the water will get very hot.** Point to the heat source and the water. **What do you want to know about the heater and the water?** Have students tell anything they might want to know about the heat source and the water. Have students respond orally, use their AAC devices to respond, or point to responses on the Student Response Guide page. Prompt students who don't have symbol use to choose any picture response. Provide feedback to students to help build meaning.	Acknowledge any response. For example, if "Will the water change colors?" is chosen, say: **It would be interesting to find out if the water will change color.** Guide students to the answer: "What will happen if we heat the water?" Say: **I would like to know what will happen if we heat the water. How about you?** On the KWHL chart, record this response in the "Want (W)" column.

Investigate and describe relationships

STEP 5

Materials	Procedure	Follow-up
• 2 measuring cups with water • Heat source • KWHL chart • Student Response Guide, page 136: **How can we find out?**	While pointing to the "W" column on the KWHL chart, restate: **We want to know what will happen if we heat the water.** Then ask: **How can we find out?** Have each student respond orally, use an AAC device to respond, point to a response on the Student Response Guide page, or pantomime turning on the heat source.	If students give alternate correct answers or incorrect answers, give a brief demo or explanation. For example, if they answer "Listen to it," let them listen for a few seconds and say: **That didn't give us much information. What else could we do?** After several students respond, acknowledge the one who answers "Heat it," or point to the preferred response and say: **I think the easiest way to find out what will happen to the water if we heat it is to heat it.** On the KWHL chart, record responses in the "How (H)" column. Circle "Heat it."

STEP 6

Materials	Procedure	Follow-up
• 2 measuring cups with water • Heat source • KWHL chart • Safety Rules for Science Class poster • Student Response Guide, page 137: **What do you think will happen?**	Review the safety rules for science listed on the poster. Be certain students understand the water in this experiment will be very hot and they need to be careful. Point to the cups of water and the heat source and say: **We'll heat one cup of water. We'll look at both cups to see what happens when we heat water. Do you think something will happen when we heat the water—yes or no?**	
	Have each student make a prediction by responding orally, using an AAC device to respond, pointing to a response on the Student Response Guide page, or nodding.	Tally the students' answers—how many said yes and how many said no—and record them in the open area at the bottom of the KWHL chart to refer to at the end of the lesson.

Investigate and describe relationships

STEP 7

Materials	Procedure	Follow-up
<ul><li>2 measuring cups with water</li><li>Heat source</li><li>Heated/Not Heated table mat</li></ul>	Say: **You just made a prediction. Some of you said yes, something will happen when we heat the water, and some of you said no. Let's find out.** Instruct one student to pour the water from one of the cups into the heat source. Have another student place the second cup of room temperature water on the table mat above the words "Not Heated." Heat the water until it boils using the heat source. Pour it back into the measuring cup and place it on the table mat above the word "Heated." Be certain steam is rising from the heated water.	Describe aloud what the students are seeing (e.g., **We're heating this water; it's getting very hot. Now I see steam coming from the water**). Encourage the students to tell what they see (e.g., "It's starting to boil"). Be sure students with visual impairments actively participate in the experiment (e.g., by listening to the heated water to hear it begin to boil). Be certain to keep the students far enough away from the steam.

STEP 8

Materials	Procedure	Follow-up
<ul><li>2 measuring cups with water on the table mat</li><li>Student Response Guide, page 138: **What's the same?**</li></ul>	Point to the cups on the table mat and say: **Here are the cups of water we used in the experiment. What's the same about both of these cups?** Have each student respond orally, use an AAC device to respond, or point to a response on the Student Response Guide page to say both cups have water in them. Prompt students who don't have symbol use to look at or touch the symbol for water after another student correctly identifies that both cups have water in them.	Praise correct responses: **Yes, there's water in both cups. That makes them the same.** If the students are not making a choice or are making an incorrect choice, guide them by saying: **There's water in both cups. That makes them the same.**

Investigate and describe relationships

STEP 9		
Materials	**Procedure**	**Follow-up**
• 2 measuring cups with water on the table mat • Student Response Guide, page 139: **What's different?**	Point to the cups on the table mat and say: **Look at the cups of water we used in the experiment. First look at the cup of water we didn't heat. Now look at the cup of water we heated. What's different about these cups?** Have each student respond orally, use an AAC device to respond, or point to a response on the Student Response Guide page to say the water is hot in one cup and one cup has steam. Prompt students who don't have symbol use to look at or touch the symbol for steam after another student correctly identifies that one cup has steam.	Praise correct responses: **Yes, the cup with water that was heated has steam going up into the air. That cup of water is evaporating. That makes the cups different.** If the students are not making a choice or are making an incorrect choice, say: **Look at the cup with hot water. The water that is heated is changing to steam. We see the steam above the cup** (point to the steam). **The cup with room temperature water is not changing to steam. It doesn't have steam above the cup. The cup with heated water is different from the cup with cool water because it's changing to steam. That makes them different.**

Construct explanation

STEP 10

Materials	Procedure	Follow-up
• 2 measuring cups with water on the table mat • Picture and word cards for evaporation • Student Response Guide, page 140: **What scientific discovery did we make?**	Read the scientific discovery statement once: **When water is heated, it turns into steam. This is called evaporation.** Say: **Let's review what we did. First we had 2 cups with water. We heated water for one cup. The other cup we left at room temperature. The water that we did not heat stayed the same. The water that we heated had steam rising from it. Evaporation is when heated water turns into steam.** Then hold up the picture and word cards for evaporation and say: **This is the picture for evaporation, and this word says evaporation. Say "evaporation."** Put the picture and word cards for evaporation in front of the cup that was heated.	
	Give students a turn to do the same (i.e., put the picture and word cards in front of the cup that was heated). For students who don't respond, have them put the picture card in front of the cup with the heated water and then guide them to match the word card. Other students may be prompted to look at the steam while you or a peer places the picture and word cards. Read the scientific discovery statement again, pointing to the words on the Student Response Guide page as you read and having the students follow along.	Give praise: **Yes, this is evaporation. This is the cup that has hot water turning into steam. The water is evaporating. Say "evaporation."**

Report

STEP 11

Materials	Procedure	Follow-up
• 2 measuring cups with water on the table mat • Picture and word cards for evaporation • KWHL chart • Student Response Guide, pages 141–142: **What did we find out?** and **Why?**	Say: **Let's review what we learned. I asked if you thought something would happen when we heated the water.** Point to the predictions on the KWHL chart. **Some of you said yes, and some of you said no. Did something happen when we heated the cup of water—yes or no?** Have each student respond orally, use an AAC device to respond, point to a response on the Student Response Guide page, or nod yes or no.	Praise the students and then summarize: **Good, something did happen. What happened was that the water that was heated turned into steam. This is called evaporation.** If any students respond "no," point to the steam and say: **Do you see steam coming from the cup with room-temperature water?** Write "Yes—water turned into steam" in the open area at the bottom of the KWHL chart.
	Point to the heated water and ask: **Why did the water turn into steam?** Have each student respond orally, use an AAC device to respond, or point to a response on the Student Response Guide page to indicate it was heated. Ask students to point to the picture and word cards for evaporation and then say "evaporation."	Point to heated water and say: **Yes, the water turned into steam because we heated it.** Scaffold for those who don't respond by saying: **What did we do to the water to turn it to steam?**

Report

STEP 12		
Materials	**Procedure**	**Follow-up**
• KWHL chart • Student Response Guide, page 143: **What did we learn?**	Say: **Let's review what we learned. When water is heated, it turns into steam. Steam is _____.** Have each student respond orally with "evaporation," use an AAC device to respond, or point to a response on the Student Response Guide page to fill in the blank.	Say: **Yes, steam is called evaporation.** Scaffold for students who say "precipitation" or "pizza" by pointing to the steam and saying: **Yes, when we heat water it turns into steam.** Write "When water is heated, it evaporates" in the "Learned (L)" column of the KWHL chart.

Review vocabulary

Materials: Picture and word cards for precipitation, evaporation, condensation, pollution, conservation

Procedure: Use the time-delay procedure to review each of the vocabulary words for the unit. See page 8 for the procedure.

Extend and review lesson

Read the story on page 49 in **ScienceWork** with the students. Help them apply the scientific concept they learned in this lesson to the story. Complete the exercise following the story together or send it home as homework.

Lesson 3 Condensation

Concept

When steam is cooled, it turns into water. This is called condensation.

Background

In this lesson, students learn more about the Earth's water cycle. They learn about the effect of temperature on water by observing steam condense into water when it's cooled.

Materials

- 2 measuring cups
- 2 metal bowls
- Timer
- Picture and word card for precipitation, evaporation, condensation, pollution, conservation
- Cooled/Not Cooled table mat (TM.pdf from the CD-ROM)
- KWHL chart
- Safety Rules for Science Class poster
- Student Response Guide, pages 144–154
- ScienceWork, pages 52–54

BRING FROM HOME Heat source (e.g., microwave, hot plate, electric pan, electric tea kettle), ice cubes, water

Preparation

Prepare for this lesson by printing the Cooled/Not Cooled table mat from the CD-ROM. Just before the lesson begins, heat enough water to fill the 2 measuring cups. Heat to the boiling point and fill the cups. Get ice cubes from a freezer and place them in one metal bowl.

Vocabulary

Review picture and sight word cards for this unit (see pages 138–140).

Engage

STEP 1		
Materials	**Procedure**	**Follow-up**
• 2 measuring cups with boiling water • 1 metal bowl of ice • 1 empty metal bowl	Engage the students by telling them: **Today in science we're going to learn more about the Earth's water cycle. We're going to learn about condensation. Let's begin our experiment. Here are some of our materials.**	
	Point to the 2 cups with hot water and the bowls. Invite the students to examine them for a few moments, make comments, and ask questions.	If students ask, "What are these?" say: **Good question.**

STEP 2		
Materials	**Procedure**	**Follow-up**
• 2 measuring cups with boiling water • 1 metal bowl of ice • 1 empty metal bowl • Student Response Guide, page 144: **What is this?**	Point to the water in the cups and the ice and ask: **What do you think these are? Make a guess.** Give each student a chance to guess before giving feedback. Remember, you do want students to make guesses in an inquiry lesson. Have each student respond orally with "cups," "water," or "ice"; use an AAC device to respond; or point to responses on the Student Response Guide page. Prompt students who don't have symbol use to look at the water and touch the picture of water in the Student Response Guide. For example, say: **You're looking at water. This is water.**	Praise correct responses. Explain: **Today we'll use water and ice in our science lesson.** If students give an incorrect answer, say: **That's a good guess.** Then give a brief reason why the choice isn't the best response. For example, for juice, say: **It looks a little bit like juice, but it's actually water.**

Engage

STEP 3		
Materials	**Procedure**	**Follow-up**
• 2 measuring cups with boiling water • 1 metal bowl of ice • 1 empty metal bowl • KWHL chart • Student Response Guide, page 145: **What do you know?**	Point to the boiling water in the cups and say: **What do you know about the material in these cups?** Have the students tell something they know about the water. Have each student respond orally, use an AAC device to respond, or point to responses on the Student Response Guide page. Prompt students who don't have symbol use to look at the cup of water and to touch the picture of "It's liquid" in the Student Response Guide. For example, say: **You're looking at the water. The water is liquid.**	Praise correct responses. Correct inappropriate answers by giving a brief reason why the response isn't the best response. For example, if "It's a solid" is chosen, say: **I don't think it's a solid. The water is liquid, and some is turning to steam.** On the KWHL chart, record the correct answers in the "Know (K)" column.

STEP 4		
Materials	**Procedure**	**Follow-up**
• 2 measuring cups with boiling water • 1 metal bowl of ice • 1 empty metal bowl • KWHL chart • Student Response Guide, page 146: **What do you want to know?**	Point to the ice and say: **This is ice. We use ice to keep things cold.** Point to the boiling water and say: **This is boiling water. It's very hot. What do you want to know about the ice and the boiling water?** Have students tell anything they might want to know about the ice and the boiling water. Have students respond orally, use their AAC devices to respond, or point to responses on the Student Response Guide page. Prompt students who don't have symbol use to choose any picture response. Provide feedback to students to help build meaning.	Acknowledge any response. For example, if "Will the ice turn colors?" is chosen, say: **It would be interesting to find out if the ice will change color.** Guide students to the answer: "What will happen if we cool down the steam with the ice?" Say: **I would like to know what will happen if we cool down the steam with the ice. How about you?** On the KWHL chart, record this response in the "Want (W)" column.

Investigate and describe relationships

STEP 5

Materials	Procedure	Follow-up
• 2 measuring cups with boiling water • 1 metal bowl of ice • 1 empty metal bowl • KWHL chart • Student Response Guide, page 147: **How can we find out?**	While pointing to the "W" column on the KWHL chart, restate: **We want to know what will happen if we cool down the steam with the ice.** Then ask: **How can we find out?** Have each student respond orally, use an AAC device to respond, point to a response on the Student Response Guide page, or pantomime what to do.	If students give alternate correct answers or incorrect answers, give a brief demo or explanation. For example, if they answer "Listen to it," let them listen for a few seconds and say: **That didn't give us much information. What else could we do?** After several students respond, acknowledge the one who answers "Put it over the steam," or point to the preferred response and say: **I think the easiest way to find out what will happen to the steam is to hold the bowl of ice over the steam.** On the KWHL chart, record responses in the "How (H)" column. Circle "Put the bowl of ice over the steam."

STEP 6

Materials	Procedure	Follow-up
• 2 measuring cups with boiling water • 1 metal bowl of ice • 1 empty metal bowl • KWHL chart • Safety Rules for Science Class poster • Student Response Guide, page 148: **What do you think will happen?**	Review the safety rules for science listed on the poster. Be certain students understand the water in this experiment will be very hot and they need to be careful. Point to the cups of boiling water, the bowl of ice, and the empty bowl and say: **We'll place the bowl of ice over a cup that has steam, and we'll place an empty bowl over the other cup with steam. We'll look to see what happens when we cool the steam. Do you think the steam will change when we cool it—yes or no?**	
	Have each student make a prediction by responding orally, using an AAC device to respond, pointing to a response on the Student Response Guide page, or nodding.	Tally the students' answers—how many said yes and how many said no—and record them in the open area at the bottom of the KWHL chart to refer to at the end of the lesson.

Investigate and describe relationships

STEP 7

Materials	Procedure	Follow-up
<ul><li>2 measuring cups with boiling water</li><li>1 metal bowl of ice</li><li>1 empty metal bowl</li><li>Timer</li><li>Cooled/Not Cooled table mat</li></ul>	Say: **You just made a prediction. Some of you said yes, the steam will change when we cool it. Some of you said no. Let's find out.** Tell one student to hold the bowl of ice over one of the cups with steaming, boiling water. Have another student hold the empty bowl over the other cup with steaming, boiling water. Use the timer to time out 1 minute and then place each bowl on the table mat above the words "Not Cooled" and "Cooled" as appropriate.	Describe aloud what the students are seeing (e.g., **We're holding the bowl of ice over the steam**). Encourage the students to tell what they see (e.g., "It's turning into water"). Be sure students with visual impairments actively participate in the experiment (e.g., by listening to the ice cubes rattling in the bowl). Be certain to keep the students far enough away from the steam.

STEP 8

Materials	Procedure	Follow-up
<ul><li>2 measuring cups with boiling water</li><li>1 metal bowl of ice</li><li>1 empty metal bowl</li><li>Cooled/Not Cooled table mat</li><li>Student Response Guide, page 149: **What's the same?**</li></ul>	Point to the materials on the table mat and the steaming cups and say: **Here are the bowl of ice, the empty bowl, and the cups of boiling water and steam we used in the experiment. What's the same about these materials?** Have each student respond orally, use an AAC device to respond, or point to a response on the Student Response Guide page to say both cups have steam and both cups have heated water. Prompt students who don't have symbol use to look at or touch the symbol for steam after another student correctly identifies that both cups have steam.	Praise correct responses: **Yes, both cups have steam. That makes them the same.** If the students are not making a choice or are making an incorrect choice, guide them by saying: **We had 2 cups with water that was heated and turned into steam. The steam coming from both cups makes them the same.**

Investigate and describe relationships

STEP 9

Materials	Procedure	Follow-up
• 2 measuring cups with boiling water • 1 metal bowl of ice • 1 empty metal bowl • Cooled/Not Cooled table mat • Student Response Guide, page 150: **What's different?**	Point to the bowl on the table mat above the word "Cooled" and say: **Look at the bowl with ice that cooled the steam. Now look at the bowl without ice that did not cool the steam** (point to the bowl on the table mat above the words "Not Cooled"). **What's different about the 2 bowls?** Have each student respond orally, use an AAC device to respond, or point to a response on the Student Response Guide page to say one bowl is cool, one is wet, and one has water on it. Prompt students who don't have symbol use to look at or touch the symbol for water after another student correctly identifies that one has water on it.	Praise correct responses: **Yes, they're different because the bowl that cooled the steam has water on its surface. That makes them different.** If the students are not making a choice or are making an incorrect choice, say: **Look at the bowl with ice. This is where the steam touched the bowl. The bowl was cool from the ice. When the steam touched the bowl cooled by the ice, it turned into water.** (Point to the outside of the bowl.) **We see the water on the outside of the bowl. The bowl that did not have ice was not cooled. The bowl without the ice does not have water on the outside. The bowl with ice is different from the empty bowl because the steam is changing into water on the outside of the bowl.**

Construct explanation

STEP 10

Materials	Procedure	Follow-up
• 2 measuring cups with boiling water • 1 metal bowl of ice • 1 empty metal bowl • Picture and word cards for condensation • Cooled/Not Cooled table mat • Student Response Guide, page 151: **What scientific discovery did we make?**	Read the scientific discovery statement once: **When steam is cooled, it turns into water. This is called condensation.** Say: **Let's review what we did. First we held the bowl with ice over the cup with steam. Next we held the empty bowl above the steam. The steam that was cooled by the ice turned into water on the outside of the bowl. The steam that was not cooled by ice did not turn into water on the outside of the bowl. Condensation is when steam is cooled and turns into water.** Then hold up the picture and word cards for condensation and say: **This is the picture for condensation, and this word says condensation. Say "condensation."** Put the picture and word card for condensation in front of the bowl with water on its surface.	
	Give students a turn to do the same (i.e., put the picture and word cards in front of the bowl with water on its surface). For students who don't respond, have them put the picture card in front of the bowl that has condensation on it and then guide them to match the word card. Other students may be prompted to look at the condensation while you or a peer places the picture and word cards. Read the scientific discovery statement again, pointing to the words on the Student Response Guide page as you read and having the students follow along.	Give praise: **Yes, this is condensation. This is the bowl that was cooled by the ice. When the steam touched the cool bowl, it turned to water. This is called condensation. Say "condensation."**

Report

STEP 11		
Materials	**Procedure**	**Follow-up**
• 2 measuring cups with boiling water • 1 metal bowl of ice • 1 empty metal bowl • Picture and word cards for condensation • KWHL chart • Student Response Guide, pages 152–153: **What did we find out?** and **Why?**	Say: Let's review what we learned. I asked if you thought the steam would change when we cooled it. Point to the predictions on the KWHL chart. Some of you said yes, and some of you said no. Did something change when we put the bowl of ice over the steam—yes or no? Have each student respond orally, use an AAC device to respond, point to a response on the Student Response Guide page, or nod yes or no.	Praise the students and then summarize: Good, the steam was cooled and turned into water. That's called condensation. If any students respond "no," point to the bowl with the water on its surface and say: Do you see the water on the outside of this bowl? Write "Yes—the steam changed to water" in the open area at the bottom of the KWHL chart.
	Point to the bowl with condensation and say: Why did the steam turn into water? Have each student respond orally, use an AAC device to respond, or point to a response on the Student Response Guide page to indicate it was cooled. Ask students to point to the picture and word cards for condensation and then say "condensation."	Point to the bowl with condensation and say: Yes, the steam turned into water because it was cooled. Scaffold for those who don't respond by saying: What did we do to the steam?

Report

STEP 12		
Materials	**Procedure**	**Follow-up**
• KWHL chart • Student Response Guide, page 154: **What did we learn?**	Say: **Let's review what we learned. When steam is cooled, it turns into water. This is called** _____. Have each student respond orally with "condensation," use an AAC device to respond, or point to a response on the Student Response Guide page to fill in the blank.	Say: **Yes, steam is called condensation.** Scaffold for students who say "pollution" or "evaporation" by pointing to the steam and saying: **When we cool steam, it turns into water.** Write "When steam is cooled, it turns into water" in the "Learned (L)" column of the KWHL chart.

Review vocabulary

Materials: Picture and word cards for precipitation, evaporation, condensation, pollution, conservation

Procedure: Use the time-delay procedure to review each of the vocabulary words for the unit. See page 8 for the procedure.

Extend and review lesson

Read the story on page 52 in **ScienceWork** with the students. Help them apply the scientific concept they learned in this lesson to the story. Complete the exercise following the story together or send it home as homework.

Lesson  Pollution

Concept

Putting something in our water that harms living things is pollution.

Background

In this lesson, students learn more about the Earth's water. They learn about a form of pollution—water pollution—and how it affects living things. They learn that pollution harms living things.

Materials

- 1 teaspoon brown tempera paint
- Plastic spoon
- Measuring cup
- 2 white feathers
- 3 plastic cups
- Picture and word card for precipitation, evaporation, condensation, pollution, conservation
- Photo of pollution
- KWHL chart
- Safety Rules for Science Class poster
- Student Response Guide, pages 155–165
- ScienceWork, pages 55–58

 Paper towels, water, cooking oil

 Feathers can be found at any craft store (such as Michaels). It's helpful if the feathers are white. Tempera paint can be found in your art department or at any craft store. Any dark color resembling oil will work.

Preparation

Prepare for this lesson by filling the 2 plastic cups with water. Put about ⅛ cup vegetable oil in the plastic cup. Add 1 teaspoon tempera paint and stir to make an oil mixture resembling crude oil.

Vocabulary

Review picture and sight word cards for this unit (see pages 138–140).

 **Engage**

STEP 1

Materials	Procedure	Follow-up
2 feathers	Engage the students by telling them: **Today in science we're going to learn more about Earth's water. We're going to learn about water pollution and the harm it does to living things. Let's begin our experiment. Here are some of our materials.**	
	Point to the 2 feathers. Invite the students to examine them for a few moments, make comments, and ask questions.	If students ask, "What are these?" say: **Good question.**

STEP 2

Materials	Procedure	Follow-up
• 2 feathers • Student Response Guide, page 155: **What is this?**	Point to the 2 feathers and ask: **What do you think these are? Make a guess.** Give each student a chance to guess before giving feedback. Remember, you do want students to make guesses in an inquiry lesson. Have each student respond orally with "feathers," use an AAC device to respond, or point to responses on the Student Response Guide page. Prompt students who don't have symbol use to look at a feather and touch the picture of the feather in the Student Response Guide. For example, say: **You're looking at a feather. This is a feather.**	Praise correct responses. If students give an incorrect answer, say: **That's a good guess.** Then give a brief reason why the choice isn't the best response. For example, for bones, say: **These help birds stay warm. They're feathers.**

Engage

STEP 3

Materials	Procedure	Follow-up
• 2 feathers • KWHL chart • Student Response Guide, page 156: **What do you know?**	Point to one of the feathers and say: **What do you know about a feather?** Have the students tell something they know about the feather. Have each student respond orally, use an AAC device to respond, or point to responses on the Student Response Guide page. Prompt students who don't have symbol use to look at the feather and to touch the picture of "It comes from a bird" in the Student Response Guide. For example, say: **You're looking at a feather. A feather comes from a bird.**	Praise correct responses. Correct inappropriate answers by giving a brief reason why the response isn't the best response. For example, if "It comes from a dog" is chosen, say: **I don't think it's from a dog. Dogs have fur. Birds have feathers. This feather comes from a bird.** On the KWHL chart, record the correct answers in the "Know (K)" column. Remind students that the feather is dry. Let the students touch the feather to feel it's dry.

STEP 4

Materials	Procedure	Follow-up
• 2 plastic cups with water • Oil-tempera paint mixture • 2 feathers • KWHL chart • Student Response Guide, page 157: **What do you want to know?**	Introduce the materials to the students. While pointing to the oil mixture, say: **This is oil. Oil is a liquid.** Pour the oil into one of the cups of water while saying: **This is a cup of water that has oil in it.** Point to the other cup of water and say: **This is a cup of water. Water is a liquid. What do you want to know about the oil, the water, and the feathers?** Have students tell anything they might want to know about the oil, the water, and the feathers. Have students respond orally, use their AAC devices to respond, or point to responses on the Student Response Guide page. Prompt students who don't have symbol use to choose any picture response. Provide feedback to students to help build meaning.	Acknowledge any response. For example, if "Will the feather disappear?" is chosen, say: **It would be interesting to find out if the feather will disappear.** Guide students to the answer: "Will both feathers be the same after we put them in the cups?" Say: **I would like to know if both feathers will be the same after we put them in the cups. How about you?** On the KWHL chart, record this response in the "Want (W)" column.

Investigate and describe relationships

STEP 5

Materials	Procedure	Follow-up
- 1 plastic cup with water - 1 plastic cup with water and oil - 2 feathers - KWHL chart - Student Response Guide, page 158: **How can we find out?**	While pointing to the "W" column on the KWHL chart, restate: **We want to know if both feathers will be the same after we put them in the cups.** Then ask: **How can we find out?** Have each student respond orally, use an AAC device to respond, point to a response on the Student Response Guide page, or pantomime putting the feathers into the cups.	If students give alternate correct answers or incorrect answers, give a brief demo or explanation. For example, if they answer "Look at the cups," let them look for a few seconds and say: **That didn't give us much information. What else could we do?** After several students respond, acknowledge the one who answers "Put a feather in each cup," or point to the preferred response and say: **I think the easiest way to find out if both feathers will be the same after we put them in the cups is to put them in the cups.** On the KWHL chart, record responses in the "How (H)" column. Circle "Put them in the cups."

STEP 6

Materials	Procedure	Follow-up
- 1 plastic cup with water - 1 plastic cup with water and oil - 2 feathers - KWHL chart - Safety Rules for Science Class poster - Student Response Guide, page 159: **What do you think will happen?**	Review the safety rules for science listed on the poster. Point to the cups of water and say: **We'll put a feather in the cup of water. Then we'll take it out, dry it, and then feel it. We'll then put another feather in the cup of water with oil. Then we'll take it out, dry it, and feel it. Do you think the feathers will look and feel the same after they are in the cups—yes or no?**	
	Have each student make a prediction by responding orally, using an AAC device to respond, pointing to a response on the Student Response Guide page, or nodding.	Tally the students' answers—how many said yes and how many said no—and record them in the open area at the bottom of the KWHL chart to refer to at the end of the lesson.

Investigate and describe relationships

STEP 7

Materials	Procedure	Follow-up
• 1 plastic cup with water • 1 plastic cup with water and oil • 2 feathers • Paper towel	Say: **You just made a prediction. Some of you said yes, the feathers will look and feel the same after they're in the cup. Some of you said no. Let's find out.** Have one student dip a feather in the cup of water. Have another student dip a feather in the cup of water with oil. Take both feathers out of the liquids. Dry them off with a paper towel. Have each student touch both feathers. The feather in the water only will be dry; the feather in the oily water will still be wet and oily.	Describe aloud what the students are seeing (e.g., **This feather feels dry, and this one feels and looks oily**). Encourage the students to tell what they see. Be sure students with visual impairments actively participate in the experiment (e.g., by placing feathers in the cups and touching the feathers). Guide them to tell you which is wet and which is dry.

STEP 8

Materials	Procedure	Follow-up
• Feather that was in oily water • Feather that was in water • Student Response Guide, page 160: **What's the same?**	Point to the feathers and say: **Here are the feathers from our experiment. What's the same about these feathers?** Have each student respond orally, use an AAC device to respond, or point to a response on the Student Response Guide page to say both were in liquid and both were dried with a towel. Prompt students who don't have symbol use to pretend to dry the feather after another student correctly identifies that both were dried with a towel.	Praise correct responses: **Yes, both feathers were in a liquid and both feathers were dried with a paper towel. That makes them the same.** If the students are not making a choice or are making an incorrect choice, guide them by saying: **Look at both of the feathers. What did we do to them both?** (Point to the cups.) **We put them both in the cups with liquid. Then what did we use to dry them?** (Point to the paper towels.) **Both of the feathers were in the liquids, and then we dried them. That makes them the same.**

Investigate and describe relationships

	STEP 9	
Materials	**Procedure**	**Follow-up**
• Feather that was in oily water • Feather that was in water • Student Response Guide, page 161: **What's different?**	Point to the feathers and say: **Now look at the feathers again. We dried both of the feathers when we took them out of the cups. What's different about these feathers?** Have each student respond orally, use an AAC device to respond, or point to a response on the Student Response Guide page to say one feather is oily and one is still wet. Prompt students who don't have symbol use to look at or touch the symbol for oily after another student correctly identifies that one feather is oily.	Praise correct responses: **Yes, one feather was in the oil. It made the feather stay wet.** If the students are not making a choice or are making an incorrect choice, say: **Remember, we put one feather in the oil and one in the water. The feather in the water dried, but the feather put in the oily water is still wet. The oil did not come off of it.** (Point to the oily feather.) **That makes them different.**

Construct explanation

STEP 10

Materials	Procedure	Follow-up
• Feather that was in oily water • Feather that was in water • Picture and word cards for pollution • Photo of pollution • Student Response Guide, page 162: **What scientific discovery did we make?**	Read the scientific discovery statement once: **Putting something in our water that harms living things is pollution.** Say: **Let's review what we did. First we put a feather in the cup of water. Then we put a feather in the cup of water with oil. We used a paper towel to dry them both off. The feather we put in the water dried right away. The feather we put in the oil did not dry. The oil did not come off. The feather stayed wet and oily** (have students touch the dry feather and then the oily feather). **Birds have feathers. If a bird swims or takes a bath in oily water, it will hurt the bird. The oil will not come off the feathers, and the bird will get sick.** Show the photo of pollution. Remind students that it's important to keep our waters clean and that other animals can be harmed by pollution too. **We can't put oil and other chemicals in our water. Putting something in our water that harms living things is pollution.** Then hold up the picture and word cards for pollution and say: **This is the picture for pollution, and this word says pollution. Say "pollution."** Put the sight word and picture card for pollution in front of the oily feather.	

(Step continues)

Construct explanation

STEP 10—*Continued*

Materials	Procedure	Follow-up
	Give students a turn to do the same (i.e., put the picture and word cards in front of the oily feather).	Give praise: **Yes, this is the wet and oily feather. The oil is harmful to the birds. Birds are living things. This oil was spilled into our water. Putting something in our water that harms living things is pollution.**
	For students who don't respond, have them put the picture card in front of the oily feather and then guide them to match the word card. Other students may be prompted to look at the oily feather while you or a peer places the picture and word cards.	
	Read the scientific discovery statement again, pointing to the words on the Student Response Guide page as you read and having the students follow along.	

Report

STEP 11

Materials	Procedure	Follow-up
• Feather that was in oily water • Feather that was in water • Picture and word cards for pollution • Photo of pollution • KWHL chart • Student Response Guide, pages 163–164: **What did we find out?** and **Why?**	Say: **Let's review what we learned. I asked you if you thought both feathers would look and feel the same after we put them in the cups. Some of you said yes, and some of you said no. Did the feathers look and feel the same—yes or no?** Have each student respond orally, use an AAC device to respond, point to a response on the Student Response Guide page, or nod yes or no.	Praise the students and then summarize: **Good, what happened is that we put the feather in a cup of water and oil. The oil was harmful and did not come off of the feather. Putting something in our water that harms living things is pollution.** If any students respond "yes," ask them to feel both feathers again. Say: **Point to the feather that is still wet and oily. The oil makes it feel oily and wet. Do both feathers feel wet?** Write "No—one feather feels wet and oily" in the open area at the bottom of the KWHL chart.
	Point to the oily feather and ask: **Why did the feather stay wet? What did the oil do to the feather?** Have each student respond orally, use an AAC device to respond, or point to a response on the Student Response Guide page to indicate the oil harmed it. Ask students to point to the picture and word cards for pollution and then say "pollution."	Point to the oily feather and say: **Yes, the oil harmed the feather.** Show the photo of pollution and point out the harmful effects of pollution. Scaffold for those who don't respond by saying: **The feather is still wet. What did the oil do to the feather?**

Report

STEP 12		
Materials	**Procedure**	**Follow-up**
• Feather that was in oily water • Feather that was in water • KWHL chart • Student Response Guide, page 165: **What did we learn?**	Say: **Let's review what we learned. Putting something in our water that harms living things is _____.** Have each student respond orally with "pollution," use an AAC device to respond, or point to a response on the Student Response Guide page to fill in the blank.	Say: **Yes, pollution harms living things.** Scaffold for students who say "cooking" or "candy" by pointing to the oily feather and saying: **Yes, putting harmful things like oil in our water is pollution.** Write "Putting something in our water that harms living things is pollution" in the "Learned (L)" column of the KWHL chart.

Review vocabulary

Materials: Picture and word cards for precipitation, evaporation, condensation, pollution, conservation

Procedure: Use the time-delay procedure to review each of the vocabulary words for the unit. See page 8 for the procedure.

Extend and review lesson

Read the story on pages 56–56 in **ScienceWork** with the students. Help them apply the scientific concept they learned in this lesson to the story. Complete the exercise following the story together or send it home as homework.

Lesson 5 Conservation

Concept

Using less water is conservation.

Background

In this lesson, students learn more about the Earth's water. They learn about conservation and a way to help conserve water.

Materials

- 1 clear plastic bowl
- 2 measuring cups
- Picture and word card for precipitation, evaporation, condensation, pollution, conservation
- **Do your part to conserve water** poster, page 101 in the ScienceWork pdf on the CD-ROM
- KWHL chart
- Safety Rules for Science Class poster
- Student Response Guide, pages 166–176
- ScienceWork, pages 59–61 and 99–101

BRING FROM HOME   Hand soap, Post-it® notes (1.5" x 2")

Preparation

Prepare for this lesson by making certain students have access to a sink and faucet. Prepare 2 Post-it® notes: one that says "water faucet running" and the other, "water faucet off."

Vocabulary

Review picture and sight word cards for this unit (see pages 138–140).

Engage

STEP 1

Materials	Procedure	Follow-up
• Sink and faucet • ScienceWork, pages 99–100: **Earth's water is important to us**	Water is very important to our lives. Let's read about how important it is. Read **Earth's water is important to us** to students and have them read along. Remind students that the lessons in this unit will help them learn how they can help save water, but they need to do their part every day. Engage the students by telling them: **Today in science we're going to learn more about the Earth's water. We're going to learn how to save water. This is called conservation. Let's begin our experiment.**	
	Point to the sink and faucet. Invite the students to examine them for a few moments, make comments, and ask questions.	If students ask, "What are these?" say: **Good question.**

STEP 2

Materials	Procedure	Follow-up
• Sink and faucet • Student Response Guide, page 166: **What is this?**	Point to the sink and faucet and ask: **What do you think these are? Make a guess.** Give each student a chance to guess before giving feedback. Remember, you do want students to make guesses in an inquiry lesson. Have each student respond orally with "a faucet" or "a sink," use an AAC device to respond, or point to responses on the Student Response Guide page. Prompt students who don't have symbol use to look at the faucet and touch the picture of a faucet in the Student Response Guide. For example, say: **You're looking at a faucet. This is a faucet.**	Praise correct responses. If students give an incorrect answer, say: **That's a good guess.** Then give a brief reason why the choice isn't the best response. For example, for "a tub," say: **It looks a little bit like a tub, but it's actually a sink. They both hold water.**

 **Engage**

STEP 3

Materials	Procedure	Follow-up
• Sink and faucet • KWHL chart • Student Response Guide, page 167: **What do you know?**	Point to the sink and the faucet and say: **What do you know about a sink and a faucet?** Have the students tell something they know about the sink and the faucet. Have each student respond orally, use an AAC device to respond, or point to responses on the Student Response Guide page. Prompt students who don't have symbol use to look at the faucet and to touch the picture of the faucet in the Student Response Guide. For example, say: **You're looking at a faucet. Water comes out of a faucet when we turn it on.**	Praise correct responses. Correct inappropriate answers by giving a brief reason why the response isn't the best response. For example, if "We swim in the sink" is chosen, say: **I don't think we swim in the sink. We wash our hands in a sink.** On the KWHL chart, record the correct answers in the "Know (K)" column.

STEP 4

Materials	Procedure	Follow-up
• Sink and faucet • Clear plastic bowl • Hand soap • KWHL chart • Student Response Guide, page 168: **What do you want to know?**	Point to the bowl, soap, sink, and faucet. Say: **What do you want to know about the bowl, soap, sink, faucet, and water?** Have students tell anything they might want to know about the bowl, soap, sink, faucet, and water. Have students respond orally, use their AAC devices to respond, or point to responses on the Student Response Guide page. Prompt students who don't have symbol use to choose any picture response. Provide feedback to students to help build meaning.	Acknowledge any response. For example, if "Will the soap change colors?" is chosen, say: **It would be interesting to find out if the soap will change colors.** Guide students to the answer: "How much water do we need to wash our hands?" Say: **I would like to know how much water we need to wash our hands. How about you?** On the KWHL chart, record this response in the "Want (W)" column.

Investigate and describe relationships

STEP 5

Materials	Procedure	Follow-up
• Sink and faucet • Clear plastic bowl • Hand soap • KWHL chart • Student Response Guide, page 169: **How can we find out?**	While pointing to the "W" column on the KWHL chart, restate: **We want to know how much water we need to wash our hands.** Then ask: **How can we find out?** Have each student respond orally, use an AAC device to respond, point to a response on the Student Response Guide page, or pantomime what to do.	If students give alternate correct answers or incorrect answers, give a brief demo or explanation. For example, if they answer "Stir the water," let them stir water in the bowl for a few seconds and say: **That didn't give us much information. What else could we do?** After several students respond, acknowledge the one who answers "Measure the water after washing our hands," or point to the preferred response and say: **I think the easiest way to find out what will happen to the water is to measure the water after we wash our hands.** On the KWHL chart, record responses in the "How (H)" column. Circle "Measure the water after washing our hands."

Investigate and describe relationships

STEP 6

Materials	Procedure	Follow-up
• Sink and faucet • Clear plastic bowl • Hand soap • KWHL chart • Safety Rules for Science Class poster • Student Response Guide, page 170: **What do you think will happen?**	Review the safety rules for science listed on the poster. Point to the sink, faucet, bowl, and hand soap, and say: **We'll turn on the faucet and wash our hands with the water and soap. First we'll leave the water running while we wash our hands. Next we'll turn the faucet off while we wash our hands and turn it on only to rinse our hands. We'll measure the water in each bowl. How much water do you think we'll use if we turn the water off while we're washing—more than if we leave it on while washing, less, or the same?**	
	Have each student make a prediction by responding orally, using an AAC device to respond, pointing to a response on the Student Response Guide page, or nodding when you say "less," "more," or "the same."	Tally the students' answers—how many said more, how many said less, and how many said the same—and record them in the open area at the bottom of the KWHL chart to refer to at the end of the lesson.

Investigate and describe relationships

STEP 7

Materials	Procedure	Follow-up
• Sink and faucet • Clear plastic bowl • Hand soap • 2 measuring cups • Prepared Post-it® notes	Say: **You just made a prediction. Some of you said we'll use more water if we turn the faucet off while we wash our hands, some of you said less, and some of you said the same. Let's find out.** Place the bowl in the sink. Have one student turn on the faucet and wash and lather his or her hands with the soap. Keep the water running while the student washes hands. Gather all the water using the bowl in the sink. When finished, take the bowl out of the sink and pour the water into a measuring cup. Add a Post-it note to the cup that says "water faucet running." Place the bowl in the sink again (make sure all water is gone). Have one student turn on the faucet and rinse his or her hands. Then turn the faucet off. Have the student use soap to lather hands, and then turn the faucet on to rinse hands. Then turn off the water again. Gather all of the water using the bowl in the sink. When finished, take the bowl out of the sink and pour it into a measuring cup to measure it. Add a Post-it note to the cup that says "water faucet off."	Describe aloud what the students are seeing. Encourage the students to tell what they see (e.g., "The bowl is full"). Be sure students with visual impairments actively participate in the experiment (e.g., by washing hands and holding both bowls to see which is heavier).

Investigate and describe relationships

STEP 8

Materials	Procedure	Follow-up
• 2 measuring cups with wash water • Student Response Guide, page 171: **What's the same?**	Point to the measuring cups and say: **Here's the water collected from the bowls. This is the water we measured. This one shows how much water we used to wash with the water running, and this one shows how much water we used when we turned the faucet on and then off. What's the same about both of these cups?** Have each student respond orally, use an AAC device to respond, or point to a response on the Student Response Guide page to say both have water in them and the water in both came from the faucet. Prompt students who don't have symbol use to look at or touch the symbol for faucet after another student correctly identifies that the water in both came from the faucet.	Praise correct responses: **Yes, there's water in both cups, and the water came from the faucet. That makes them the same.** If the students are not making a choice or are making an incorrect choice, guide them by saying: **Look at both cups. What's in both cups? Yes, water. That makes them the same.**

STEP 9

Materials	Procedure	Follow-up
• 2 measuring cups with wash water • Student Response Guide, page 172: **What's different?**	Point to the measuring cups and say: **Look at the water we collected again. This is the water we measured. We measured the water we used while the faucet was on and then off. What's different about these cups?** Have each student respond orally, use an AAC device to respond, or point to a response on the Student Response Guide page to say the cups have different amounts of water. Prompt students who don't have symbol use to look at or touch the cup with less water after another student correctly identifies that the cups have different amounts of water.	Praise correct responses: **Yes, the amount of water is different. One cup has less water in it than the other because we turned the water off while washing our hands. That makes them different.** If the students are not making a choice or are making an incorrect choice, say: **Look at the cups. We left the water on the first time we washed our hands.** (Point to the cup with more water.) **What did we do with the faucet when we washed our hands the second time?** (Point to the cup with less water.) **We turned the faucet off. We used less water. That makes them different.**

Construct explanation

Materials	Procedure	Follow-up
• 2 measuring cups with wash water • Picture and word cards for conservation • Student Response Guide, page 173: **What scientific discovery did we make?**	Read the scientific discovery statement once: **Using less water is conservation.** Say: **Let's review what we did. First we turned on the water and washed our hands.** (Point to the cup with the most water.) **Then we washed our hands with a little bit of water. We turned off the faucet while we washed, and turned it back on to rinse our hands.** (Point to the cup with the least water.) **We measured the amount of water in each bowl and found out that when we leave the water on while we wash our hands, we use more water. When we turn off the water while we wash our hands, we use less water. Using less water is conservation.** Then hold up the picture and word cards for conservation and say: **This is the picture for conservation, and this word says conservation. Say "conservation."** Put the picture and word cards for conservation in front of the cup holding the most water.	
	Give students a turn to do the same (i.e., put the picture and word cards in front of the cup with the most water). For students who don't respond, have them put the picture card in front of the cup with less water and then guide them to match the word card. Other students may be prompted to look at the cup with less water while you or a peer places the picture and word cards. Read the scientific discovery statement again, pointing to the words on the Student Response Guide page as you read and having the students follow along.	Give praise: **Yes, this is the cup that shows we used less water. Using less water is conservation. Say "conservation."**

Report

STEP 11

Materials	Procedure	Follow-up
• 2 measuring cups with wash water • Picture and word cards for conservation • KWHL chart • Student Response Guide, pages 174–175: **What did we find out?** and **Why?**	Say: **Let's review what we learned. I asked you if you thought that when we turn off the water while washing our hands, we would use more, less, or the same amount of water. Point to the predictions on the KWHL chart. Some of you said more, some of you said less, and some of you said we would use the same amount of water. When we turned the water off while washing our hands, how much water did we use—more, less, or the same?** Have each student respond orally, use an AAC device to respond, point to a response on the Student Response Guide page, or nod yes or no.	Praise the students and then summarize: **Good, what happened is that when we turned the water off, we used less water. So we learned that turning off the faucet uses less water.** If any students say "more" or "the same," point to the cups and remind them what the cup measures. Then ask: **Does this have more or less water in it?** Write "Less water—faucet off while washing hands" in the open area at the bottom of the KWHL chart.
	Point to cups and say: **Why did we use less water?** Have each student respond orally, use an AAC device to respond, or point to a response on the Student Response Guide page to indicate the faucet was off. Ask students to point to the picture and word cards for conservation and then say "conservation."	Point to the cup with less water and say: **Yes, we used less water because the faucet was off. The water was not running. That is conservation.** Scaffold for those who don't respond by saying: **What did you do with the faucet when you used less water?**

Report

STEP 12		
Materials	**Procedure**	**Follow-up**
• ScienceWork, page 101: **Do your part to conserve water** poster • KWHL chart • Student Response Guide, page 176: **What did we learn?**	Say: **Let's review what we learned. Conservation is using** _____. Have each student respond orally with "less water," use an AAC device to respond, or point to a response on the Student Response Guide page to fill in the blank. Review the **Do your part to conserve water** poster with students. Read the poster together and then have the students take their poster home to share with their families.	Say: **Yes, conservation is using less water.** Scaffold for students who say "more water" or "mud" by pointing to the cup with less water and saying: **One cup shows more water, but this one shows less water and none of them shows mud.** Write "Conservation is using less water" in the "Learned (L)" column of the KWHL chart.

Review vocabulary

Materials: Picture and word cards for precipitation, evaporation, condensation, pollution, conservation

Procedure: Use the time-delay procedure to review each of the vocabulary words for the unit. See page 8 for the procedure.

Extend and review lesson

Read the story on page 59 in **ScienceWork** with the students. Help them apply the scientific concept they learned in this lesson to the story. Complete the exercise following the story together or send it home as homework.

Unit D Chemistry

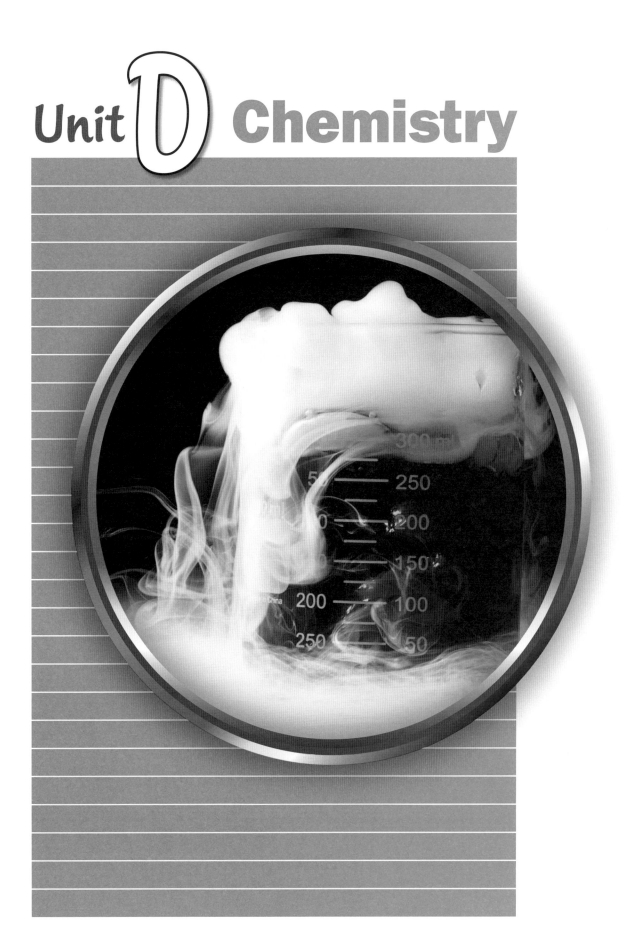

Lesson 1 Solutions

Concept

A solute plus a solvent equals a solution.

Background

In this lesson, students learn about solutions. They discover how a solute and solvent create a solution. Although many chemicals are comprised of solutes and solvents, for safety, this lesson uses powdered drink mix and water. **Do not** tell the students what the powdered mix is. Treat it as you would a dangerous chemical to teach caution with unknown chemicals.

Materials

- 3 clear plastic cups
- Plastic spoon
- Picture and word cards for solute, solvent, solution, chemical reaction
- KWHL chart
- Safety Rules for Science Class poster
- Student Response Guide, pages 178–188
- ScienceWork, pages 64–66

BRING FROM HOME

Water, 4 packets of red powdered drink mix

TO REPLENISH MATERIALS

Any dissolvable, colored powder can be used in this experiment, including Kool-Aid® and tempera paint.

Preparation

Add 4 packets of powdered drink mix to 1 cup. Fill the other 2 cups about half full of water.

Vocabulary

Teach picture symbols and sight words for this unit (see pages 189–191) to familiarize students with the vocabulary introduced in this lesson.

 Engage

STEP 1		
Materials	**Procedure**	**Follow-up**
3 plastic cups: • 1 with red powder • 2 with water	Engage the students by telling them: **Today in science we're going to learn about solutes, solvents, and solutions. You'll find out that we use solutions every day.**	
	Show the cups to the students and invite them to examine the materials for a few moments, make comments, and ask questions.	If students ask, "What are these?" say: **Good question.**

STEP 2		
Materials	**Procedure**	**Follow-up**

• 3 plastic cups:
  • 1 with red powder
  • 2 with water
• Student Response Guide, page 178: **What is this?**
	Hold up each cup individually and ask: **What do you think is in this cup? Make a guess.** Give each student a chance to guess before giving feedback. Remember, you do want students to make guesses in an inquiry lesson.
	
	Have each student respond orally with "powder," "liquid," or "water"; use an AAC device to respond; or point to responses in the Student Response Guide.
	
	Prompt students who don't have symbol use to look at a cup and to touch the picture in the Student Response Guide. For example, say: **You're looking at water. This is water.**
		Praise correct responses. If students give an incorrect answer, say: **That's a good guess.** Then give a brief reason why the choice isn't the best response. For example, for "sand," say: **That's a good guess. It looks a bit like sand, but it's actually powder.**

Engage

STEP 3

Materials	Procedure	Follow-up

• 3 plastic cups:
  • 1 with red powder
  • 2 with water
• KWHL chart
• Student Response Guide, page 179:
What do you know?
	Point to the cup with the powder and ask: **What do you know about what's in this cup?** Have the students tell something they know about what's in the cup.
	
	Have each student respond orally, use an AAC device to respond, or point to responses in the Student Response Guide.
	
	Prompt students who don't have symbol use to look at each cup and to touch the picture of "It's dry" in the Student Response Guide. For example, say: **You're looking at the powder. It's dry.**
	
	Repeat with a cup that has water in it.
		Praise correct responses.
		
		Correct inappropriate answers by giving a brief reason why the response isn't the best response. For example, if "It's old" is chosen, say: **I don't think we know if it's old. It could be new.**
		
		On the KWHL chart, record the correct answers under the "Know (K)" column. Draw a line to separate the responses for the powder versus the water.

STEP 4

Materials	Procedure	Follow-up

• 3 plastic cups:
  • 1 with red powder
  • 2 with water
• KWHL chart
• Student Response Guide, page 180:
What do you want to know?
	Point to the cups and ask: **What do you want to know about what's in these cups?**
	
	Have students tell anything they want to know about the powder and the water.
	
	Have students respond orally, use their AAC devices to respond, or point to responses in the Student Response Guide.
	
	Prompt students who don't have symbol use to chose any picture response. Provide feedback to students to help build meaning.
		Acknowledge any response. For example, if "How much do they cost?" or "How old are they?" are chosen, say: **It would be interesting to find out how much they cost or how old they are.**
		
		Guide students to the answer: "What if we mix them together?" Say: **I would like to know what happens if we mix them together. How about you?**
		
		On the KWHL chart, record this response in the "Want (W)" column.

Investigate and describe relationships

STEP 5

Materials	Procedure	Follow-up
• KWHL chart • Student Response Guide, page 181: **How can we find out?**	While pointing to the W column on the KWHL chart, restate: **We want to know what happens if we mix them together.** Then ask: **How can we find out?** Have each student respond orally, use their AAC device to respond, point to a response in the Student Response Guide, or pantomime a stirring action.	If students give alternate correct answers or incorrect answers, give a brief demo or explanation. For example, if they answer "Look at them," let them look at the cups and say: **That didn't give us much information. What else could we do?** After several students respond, acknowledge the one who answers "Mix them," or point to the preferred response and say: **I think the easiest way to find out is to mix them.** On the KWHL chart, record responses in the "How (H)" column. Circle "Mix them."

STEP 6

Materials	Procedure	Follow-up

• 3 plastic cups:
  • 1 with red powder
  • 2 with water
• KWHL chart
• Safety Rules for Science Class poster
• Student Response Guide, page 182: **What do you think will happen?**
	Review the safety rules for science listed on the poster.
	
	Say: **When you mix a powder with a liquid, sometimes the liquid changes. Sometimes it doesn't. Do you think the water will change when we mix the powder with it— yes or no?**	

	Have each student make a prediction by responding orally, using their AAC device to respond, pointing to a response in the Student Response Guide, or nodding.	Tally the students' answers— how many said yes and how many said no—and record them in the open area at the bottom of the KWHL chart to refer to at the end of the lesson.

Investigate and describe relationships

STEP 7

Materials	Procedure	Follow-up

• 3 plastic cups:
  • 1 with red powder
  • 2 with water
• Plastic spoon
	Say: **You each just made a prediction. Some of you said yes, the water will change, and some said no. Let's find out if the water will change.**
	
	Instruct one student to put a spoonful of the powder in one of the cups of water and have another use a spoon to stir it. Have other students observe the experiment.
		Describe aloud what happens, and encourage the students to tell what they see (e.g., "It's turning red"). Be sure students with visual impairments actively participate in the experiment (e.g., by stirring the mixture).

STEP 8

Materials	Procedure	Follow-up

• 2 cups:
  • with clear water
  • with water and powder mix
• Student Response Guide, page 183: **What's the same?**
	Hold up the cup with the clear water and say: **Here's what our science material looked like before we did our experiment—before we added the powder.** Then hold up the cup with the dissolved powder and say: **Here's what the material looks like after the experiment. Let's compare them. What's the same about the materials?**
	
	Have each student respond orally, use their AAC device to respond, or point to a response on the Student Response Page to say they are both liquids.
	
	Prompt students who don't have symbol use to look at or touch the 2 liquids after another student correctly identifies that they are both liquids.
		Praise correct responses: **Yes, they're both liquids. That makes them the same.**
		
		If students are not making a choice or are making an incorrect choice, guide them by saying: **What's in both of the cups?** Point to the cup with clear water and say: **Here's the water. Remember, water is a type of liquid. Is there liquid in this cup?** Point to the cup with the dissolved powder and say: **Here's the water mixed with the powder. Is there liquid in this cup?**
		
		Explain: **There was liquid in this cup before we mixed the powder in, and there is still liquid after we mixed in the powder.**

Investigate and describe relationships

	STEP 9	
Materials	**Procedure**	**Follow-up**
• 3 cups: • with powder • with clear water • with powder and water combined • Student Response Guide, page 184: **What's different?**	Hold up the cup with the clear water and say: **Here's what our science material looked like before we did our experiment—before we added the powder.** Then hold up the cup with the dissolved powder and say: **Here's what the material looks like after the experiment. Let's compare them. What's different about the materials?** Have each student respond orally, use their AAC device to respond, or point to a response in the Student Response Guide to say they're different colors. Prompt students who don't have symbol use to look at or touch the colored liquid after another student correctly identifies that they're different colors.	Praise correct responses: **Yes, they're different colors.** If students are not making a choice or are making an incorrect choice, guide them by pointing to the cup with the dissolved powder and say: **Here's the water mixed with powder. What color is the liquid in this cup? Here's the water before we mixed it with the powder. Are the colors different or the same?**

Construct explanation

STEP 10

Materials	Procedure	Follow-up
<ul><li>3 cups:<ul><li>with powder</li><li>with clear water</li><li>with powder and water combined</li></ul></li><li>Picture and word cards for solute, solvent, solution</li><li>Student Response Page 185: **What scientific discovery did we make?**</li></ul>	Read the scientific discovery statement once: **A solute plus a solvent equals a solution.** Say: **Let's review what we did. We had a powder in the cup. We call that powder a solute. A solute is something we can mix with liquid.** Hold up the picture and word cards for solute and place them in front of the cup with the remaining powder. Say: **This is the picture for solute and this word says solute.**	
	Give students a turn to do the same (i.e., put the picture and word cards in front of the cup with the remaining powder). For students who don't respond, have them put the picture card with the cup and then guide them to match the word card. Other students may be prompted to look at the cup with powder while you or a peer places the picture and word cards. Say: **We also had a cup with water, a solvent. A solvent is a liquid you can mix with a solute.** Hold up the picture and word cards for solvent and place them in front of the cup with the clear water. Say: **This is the picture for solvent, and this word says solvent.**	Give praise: **Yes, solute. A solute is a powder that can be mixed with a liquid. The powder is a solute.**
	Give students a turn to do the same (i.e., put the picture and word cards in front of the cup with the clear water). For students who don't respond, have them put the picture card with the clear water cup and then guide them to match the word card. Other students may be prompted to look at the cup with clear water while you or a peer places the picture and word cards.	Give praise: **Good, this is the solvent. The solvent is liquid. The water is liquid. The water is a solvent.**

(Step continues)

Construct explanation

Materials	Procedure	Follow-up
	Point to the cup with the red liquid and say: **Then we mixed the powder and the water together and got this. This is a solution. When you mix a solute with a solvent, you get a solution.** Hold up the picture and word cards for solution and place them in front of the cup with the red liquid. Say: **This is the picture for solution, and this word says solution.**	
	Give students a turn to do the same (i.e., put the picture and word cards in front of the cup with the red liquid). For students who don't respond, have them put the picture card with the cup and then guide them to match the word card. Other students may be prompted to look at the cup with red liquid while you or a peer places the picture and word cards. Read the scientific discovery statement again, pointing to the words on the Student Response Guide page as you read and having the students follow along.	Give praise: **Yes, solution. A solute and a solvent create a solution.**

Report

STEP 11

Materials	Procedure	Follow-up
• 3 cups: • with powder • with clear water • with powder and water combined • Picture and word cards for solute, solvent, solution • KWHL chart • Student Response Guide, pages 186–187: **What did we find out?** and **Why?**	Say: **Let's review what we found out. I asked you if the water would change when we mixed it with the powder.** Point to the predictions on the KWHL chart. **Some of you said yes, and some said no. Did the water change?** Have each student respond orally, use their AAC device to respond, point to a response in the Student Response Guide, or nod yes or no.	Praise the students and then summarize: **Good, the water did change colors, so we learned that yes, it changed. The solute—the powder—was mixed with the solvent—the water—to become this solution.** If any students respond "no," show them the before and after cups. Write "Yes—change" in the open area at the bottom of the KWHL chart.
	Point to the cup with the solution and ask: **Why did the water change colors?** Have each student respond orally, use their AAC device to respond, or point to a response in the Student Response Guide to indicate that the water changed because a solute was added.	If students don't answer correctly, rephrase the question: **What made it change?** or **Point to what made it change.** Scaffold for students who say "A book was added" or "A solvent was added" by rephrasing the question: **What did we add to the solvent?**

STEP 12

Materials	Procedure	Follow-up
• KWHL chart • Student Response Guide, page 188: **What did we learn?**	Say: **Let's review what we learned. What happens when you mix a solute with a solvent? A solute plus a solvent equals a _____.** Have each student respond orally with "solution," use an AAC device to respond, or point to the response in the Student Response Guide to fill in the blank.	Say: **Yes, a solute plus a solvent makes a solution.** Scaffold for students who say "bread" or "Earth" by rephrasing the question: **What do we call the red liquid?** Write "A solute plus a solvent equals a solution" in the "Learned (L)" column of the KWHL chart.

Teach vocabulary

Materials	Procedure	Follow-up
Picture cards: • solute • solvent • solution • chemical reaction	Review the picture cards with students individually when possible. In this first round, give the student a prompt without delay (zero time delay). Place the picture cards in front of the student. Say: **Show me (solute)** and point to the card as you ask the student to point (zero time delay). Shuffle the cards. Repeat this procedure for the remaining 3 cards.	If student points correctly, give praise: **Good! You pointed to (solute).** If student doesn't point, provide physical guidance to point.
	In this second round of vocabulary review, give the student up to 5 seconds to respond independently (5-second time delay). Shuffle the picture cards, place them in front of the student, and say: **Point to (solute).** Repeat this process for the remaining 3 cards.	If the student points correctly, give praise: **Good! You pointed to (solute) by yourself. Say (solute).** If the student doesn't point, model pointing and say: **This is (solute). Point to (solute). Say (solute).** If the student makes an error, point to the correct answer and say: **This is (solute). Point to (solute). Say (solute).** Shuffle the cards and repeat this process for the remaining 3 cards.

Teach vocabulary

Materials	Procedure	Follow-up
Word cards: • solute • solvent • solution • chemical reaction	Review the word cards with students individually if possible. In this first round, give the student a prompt without delay (zero time delay). Place the word cards in front of the student. Say: **Show me (solute)** and point to the card as you ask the student to point (zero time delay). Shuffle the cards. Repeat this procedure for the remaining 3 cards.	If the student points correctly, give praise: **Good! You pointed to (solute). Say (solute).** If the student doesn't point, provide physical guidance to point.
	In this second round of vocabulary review, give the student up to 5 seconds to respond independently (5-second time delay). Shuffle the word cards, place them in front of the student, and say: **Point to (solute).** Repeat this process for the remaining 3 cards.	If the student points correctly, give praise: **Good! You pointed to (solute) by yourself. Say (solute).** If the student doesn't point, model pointing and say: **This is (solute). Point to (solute). Say (solute).** If the student makes an error, point to the correct answer and say: **This is (solute). Point to (solute). Say (solute).** Shuffle the cards and repeat this process for the remaining 3 cards.

Teach vocabulary

Materials	Procedure	Follow-up
Picture and word cards: • solute • solvent • solution • chemical reaction	In the first round, place the word cards in front of the student. Then hand a picture card to the student and say: **Match this picture to the word.** Match the picture card to the word card as you ask the student to match them (zero time delay). Shuffle the cards. Repeat this procedure for the remaining 3 cards.	If the student matches correctly, give praise: **Good! You matched the picture to the word. Say (solute).** If the student doesn't match the cards, provide physical guidance to point.
	In a second round, give the student up to 5 seconds to match 2 cards independently (5-second time delay). Repeat this process for the remaining 3 cards.	If the student matches correctly, give praise: **Good! You matched the two cards by yourself. Say (solute).** If the student doesn't match the cards, model matching and say: **This is (solute). Match this card to the word (solute). Say (solute).** If the student makes an error, point to the correct answer and say: **This is (solute). Match this card to (solute). Say (solute).** Shuffle the cards and repeat this process for the remaining 3 cards.

Reviewing vocabulary in a group

If reviewing vocabulary in a group, follow the format described, but have one student respond while you cue the others to watch. Pick a second student at random to repeat the response from time to time to be sure everyone is watching.

Extend and review lesson

Read the story on page 64 in **ScienceWork** with the students. Help them apply the scientific concept they learned in this lesson to the story. Complete the exercise following the story together or send it home as homework.

Lesson 2 Chemical reactions

Concept

Some mixtures have a chemical reaction.

Background

In this lesson, students learn more about solutions. They learn that mixing different materials together can produce a chemical reaction. The lesson begins with an explanation of what a chemical reaction looks like. For safety, this lesson uses vinegar, baking soda, salt, and flour for the experiment. Treat the solutions as you would dangerous chemicals to teach students to be cautious with all chemicals and materials.

Materials

- 3 clear plastic cups and 1 plastic spoon for each student and for demonstration
- Picture and word cards for solute, solvent, solution, chemical reaction
- KWHL chart
- Safety Rules for Science Class poster
- Student Response Guide, pages 189–199
- ScienceWork, pages 67–69 and 102–103

BRING FROM HOME Small bag of flour, container of salt, box of baking soda, gallon of vinegar, permanent marker, 3 large zip-tight plastic bags

Preparation

Partially fill 3 zip-tight plastic bags with the solid materials and set them next to the packages (e.g., place the plastic bag with salt next to the container of salt) in your work area. Using a permanent marker, write S, B, or F on the cups so each student will have a set of each.

Vocabulary

Review picture and sight word cards for this unit (see pages 189–191).

 **Engage**

STEP 1		
Materials	**Procedure**	**Follow-up**
• Bags of flour, salt, baking soda • ScienceWork, pages 102–103: **What is a chemical reaction?**	Engage the students by telling them: **Today in science we're going to see that when we mix some solutes with solvents, the materials mixed could have a chemical reaction. Before we begin our experiment, let's talk about what a chemical reaction is. What will it look like?** Read pages 102–103 in ScienceWork and have the students follow along. Point out that when a chemical reaction happens, they'll be able to see a change, and sometimes they'll be able to hear the change (as in bubbling).	
	Let's begin our experiment. Here are some of our materials. Open the bags so students are able to see the consistency of the materials. Show the bags to the students and invite them to examine the materials for a few moments, make comments, and ask questions.	If students ask, "What are these?" say: **Good question.**

Engage

	STEP 2	
Materials	**Procedure**	**Follow-up**
• Bags of flour, salt, baking soda • Vinegar • Picture and word cards for solute and solvent • Student Response Guide, page 189: **What is this?**	Hold up each bag one at a time and ask: **What do you think is in this bag? Make a guess.** Give each student a chance to guess before giving feedback. Remember, you do want students to make guesses in an inquiry lesson. Have each student respond orally with "salt," "flour," or "baking soda"; use an AAC device to respond; or point to responses on the Student Response Guide page. Prompt students who don't have symbol use to look at the contents of the bags and to touch the pictures in the Student Response Guide. For example, say: **You're looking at salt. This is salt.** Review the concept of solute. While holding the bags, say: **This is flour. This is salt. This is baking soda. They are solids and are the solutes for our experiment today.** Then hold up the picture and word cards for solute and say: **This is the picture for solute, and this is the word solute. Say "solute."** Hold up the vinegar and introduce it as a solvent. Say: **I have one more material to show you. This is vinegar. Vinegar is a liquid, and it is the solvent for our experiment today.** Then hold up the picture and cards for solvent and say: **This is the picture for solvent, and this word says solvent. Say "solvent."**	Praise correct responses. If students give an incorrect answer, say: **That's a good guess.** Then give a brief reason why the choice is not the best response. For example, for "sand," say: **That's a good guess. It looks a bit like sand, but it's actually flour.**

 **Engage**

STEP 3		
Materials	**Procedure**	**Follow-up**
<ul><li>Bags of flour, salt, baking soda</li><li>Vinegar</li><li>KWHL chart</li><li>Student Response Guide, page 190: **What do you know?**</li></ul>	Point to the flour and ask: **What do you know about what's in this bag?** Have the students tell something they know about the flour. Have each student respond orally, use an AAC device to respond, or point to responses on the Student Response Guide page. Prompt students who don't have symbol use to look at the contents of the bag and to touch the picture of "It's dry" in the Student Response Guide. For example, say: **You're looking at flour. Flour is dry.** Repeat the question for the baking soda, then the salt, and then the vinegar.	Praise correct responses. Correct inappropriate answers by giving a brief reason why the response isn't the best response. For example, if "It's loud" is chosen, say: **I don't think it makes a sound. Do you hear it?** On the KWHL chart, record the correct answers in the "Know (K)" column. Draw a line to separate the responses for each: the flour, the baking soda, the salt, and the vinegar.

STEP 4		
Materials	**Procedure**	**Follow-up**
<ul><li>Bags of flour, salt, baking soda</li><li>KWHL chart</li><li>Student Response Guide, page 191: **What do you want to know?**</li></ul>	Point to the materials and ask: **What do you want to know about the liquid and these solids?** Have students tell anything they might want to know about the materials. Have students respond orally, use their AAC devices to respond, or point to responses on the Student Response Guide page. Prompt students who don't have symbol use to choose any picture response. Provide feedback to students to help build meaning.	Acknowledge any response. For example, if "What colors are they?" is chosen, say: **It's easy to tell what color they are.** Guide students to the answer: "What will happen if we mix them together?" Say: **I would like to know what will happen if we mix them together. How about you?** On the KWHL chart, record this response in the "Want (W)" column.

Investigate and describe relationships

STEP 5

Materials	Procedure	Follow-up
• KWHL chart • Student Response Guide, page 192: **How can we find out?**	While pointing to the "W" column on the KWHL chart, restate: **We want to know what happens if we mix them together.** Then ask: **How can we find out?** Have each student respond orally, use an AAC device to respond, point to a response on the Student Response Guide page, or pantomime a stirring action.	If students give alternate correct answers or incorrect answers, give a brief demo or explanation. For example, if they answer "Look at them," let them look at the bags and say: **That didn't give us much information. What else could we do?** After several students respond, acknowledge the one who answers "Mix them," or point to the preferred response and say: **I think the easiest way to find out is to mix them.** On the KWHL chart, record responses in the "How (H)" column. Circle "Mix them."

Investigate and describe relationships

STEP 6

Materials	Procedure	Follow-up
• 3 marked cups and 1 spoon per student • Vinegar • Bag of flour, container of salt, box of baking soda • Picture and word cards for chemical reaction • Safety Rules for Science Class poster • Student Response Guide, page 193: **What do you think will happen?**	Review the safety rules for science listed on the poster. Distribute a set of the 3 marked cups and a spoon to each student. Fill each cup ⅓ full of vinegar. Say: **We're going to put vinegar into each of the cups and see what happens when we mix different materials— different solutes—with the vinegar. When materials are mixed together and make a big change, that change is called a chemical reaction. We'll find out if the different materials will have a chemical reaction with the vinegar.** Then hold up the picture and word cards for chemical reaction and say: **This is the picture for chemical reaction, and these words say chemical reaction. Say "chemical reaction."** Line up your own set of cups of vinegar and place one solid in front of each cup to show students what will be mixed with the vinegar. **Do you think the solutes will have the same reaction when we mix them with the solvent—yes or no?**	
	Have each student make a prediction by responding orally, using an AAC device to respond, pointing to a response on the Student Response Guide page, or nodding.	Tally the students' answers—how many said yes and how many said no—and record them in the open area at the bottom of the KWHL chart to refer to at the end of the lesson.

Investigate and describe relationships

STEP 7		
Materials	**Procedure**	**Follow-up**
• 3 cups with vinegar and 1 spoon per student • Bags of salt, flour, baking soda	Say: **You each just made a prediction. Some of you said yes, the materials will all have the same reaction when they're mixed with the vinegar, and some of you said no. Let's find out.** Provide salt for each student. Instruct each student to put some salt in the cup marked S (or you can add this to the cup for the student). Then have the student stir it and observe the (lack of) reaction. Repeat for the flour, having the student place the flour in the cup marked F, stir the mixture, and observe the (lack of) reaction. Finally, repeat for the baking soda, having the student place the baking soda in the cup marked B, stir the mixture, and observe the reaction.	Describe aloud what happens, and encourage the students to tell what they see (e.g., "Nothing is happening," or "It's bubbling"). Be sure students with visual impairments actively participate in the experiment (e.g., by stirring the mixture or by hearing you describe what's happening). When placing the baking soda in the vinegar solvent, say: **Do you notice the bubbles? The vinegar and the baking soda just had a chemical reaction.**

STEP 8		
Materials	**Procedure**	**Follow-up**
• The cups with the solutions • Student Response Guide, page 194: **What's the same?**	Hold up the cups, one at a time and say: **Here's one of the solutions from the experiment—the vinegar and the salt. Here's another solution from the experiment—the vinegar and the flour. Here's another solution from the experiment—the vinegar and the baking soda. What's the same about these solutions?** Have each student respond orally, use an AAC device to respond, or point to a response on the Student Response Guide page to say they are all solutions and they are all liquids. Prompt students who don't have symbol use to look at or touch the cups with the 3 solutions after another student correctly identifies that the materials are solutions.	Praise correct responses: **Yes, they are all liquids and solutions. That makes them the same.** If the students are not making a choice or are making an incorrect choice, hold up one cup at a time and say: **What's in this cup? Remember we added vinegar to all the cups. Then we added something else to each one.** (Point to the materials that were added.) **We mixed the materials into the vinegar to make these solutions. These are all solutions. That makes them the same. And they are all liquids** (jiggle the cup to show the solutions are liquid).

Investigate and describe relationships

STEP 9		
Materials	**Procedure**	**Follow-up**
<ul><li>The cups with the solutions</li><li>Student Response Guide, page 195: **What's different?**</li></ul>	Hold up the cups one at a time and say: **Look again. Here's one of the solutions from the experiment—the vinegar and the salt. Here's another one—the vinegar and the flour. Here's another one—the vinegar and the baking soda. What's different about the mixtures in these solutions?** Have each student respond orally, use an AAC device to respond, or point to a response on the Student Response Guide page to say one had a bubbly reaction. Prompt students who don't have symbol use to look at or touch the solution with the bubbles and then touch one without bubbles.	Praise correct responses: **Yes, one had a bubbly reaction and the others didn't. That makes this one different.** If the students are not making a choice or are making an incorrect choice, hold up one cup at a time and say: **Let's look at all the cups. When we added the flour to the vinegar, we didn't see a reaction. When we added the salt, we didn't see a reaction. When we added the baking soda, we did see a chemical reaction. Only the baking soda and vinegar made a chemical reaction by bubbling. The bubbly reaction was different for this solution.**

Construct explanation

STEP 10

Materials	Procedure	Follow-up
• The cups with the solutions • Picture and word cards for chemical reaction • Student Response Guide, page 196: **What scientific discovery did we make?**	Read the scientific discovery statement once: **Some mixtures have a chemical reaction.** Say: **Let's review what we did. First we poured the liquid vinegar into the cups. Then we added some solutes—the flour to this cup, the salt to this cup, and the baking soda to this cup. We mixed the solutes with the vinegar and made different solutions. And we watched to see if any of the mixtures had a chemical reaction.** Put the picture and word cards for chemical reaction in front of the mixture that had a chemical reaction.	
	Give students a turn to do the same (i.e., put the picture and word cards in front of their solution that had a chemical reaction). For students who don't respond, have them put the picture card with the materials and then guide them to match the word card. Other students may be prompted to look at the solution while you or a peer places the picture and word cards. Read the scientific discovery statement again, pointing to the words on the Student Response Guide page as you read and having the students follow along.	Give praise: **Yes, this is the solution that had a chemical reaction. Say "chemical reaction."**

Report

STEP 11

Materials	Procedure	Follow-up
• Picture and word cards for chemical reaction • KWHL chart • Student Response Guide, pages 197–198: **What did we find out?** and **Why?**	Say: **Let's review what we found out. I asked you if you thought the solutes would have the same reaction when we mixed them with the vinegar solvent.** Point to the predictions on the KWHL chart. **Some of you said yes, and some said no. Did all the solutes have a chemical reaction when we mixed them with the solvent?** Have each student respond orally, use an AAC device to respond, or point to a response on the Student Response Guide page, or nod yes or no.	Praise the students and then summarize: **No, the mixtures didn't all react the same way. One of the mixtures bubbled, and the others did not.** If any students respond yes, show the solutions and add a little more baking soda to the cup marked B. Write "Yes—change" in the open area at the bottom of the KWHL chart.
	Point to the mixture marked B and ask: **Why did the mixture in one cup bubble?** Have each student respond orally, use an AAC device to respond, or point to a response on the Student Response Guide page to indicate that the mixture bubbled because there was a chemical reaction. Ask students to point to the picture and word cards for chemical reaction, then say "chemical reaction."	Point to the B mixture and say: **Yes, this mixture bubbled because there was a chemical reaction.** Scaffold for those who don't respond by asking: **Which mixture bubbled?** Or point to the cup marked B and say: **This mixture had a chemical reaction.**

Report

STEP 12		
Materials	**Procedure**	**Follow-up**
• KWHL chart • Student Response Guide, page 199: **What did we learn?**	Say: **Let's review what we learned. What can happen when you mix materials? Some mixtures have a** _____**.** Have each student respond orally with "chemical reaction," use an AAC device to respond, or point to a response on the Student Response Guide page to fill in the blank.	Say: **Yes, some mixtures have a chemical reaction. We put different solutes in each cup, and one had a chemical reaction.** Scaffold for students who say "laugh" or "pizza" by rephrasing the question: **What did we say happened when the materials bubbled?** Write "Some mixtures have a chemical reaction" in the "Learned (L)" column of the KWHL chart.

Review vocabulary

Materials: Picture and word cards for solute, solvent, solution, chemical reaction

Procedure: Use the time-delay procedure to review each of the vocabulary words for the unit. See page 8 for the procedure.

Extend and review lesson

Read the story on page 67 in **ScienceWork** with the students. Help them apply the scientific concept they learned in this lesson to the story. Complete the exercise following the story together or send it home as homework.

Lesson 3 Solutions and chemical reactions

Concept

Solutions can cause different chemical reactions.

Background

In this lesson, students learn that solutions can cause different chemical reactions. They'll learn that the same solution causes a dirty penny to look clean and an iron nail to look dirty. To help students compare what happens before and after the experiment, an extra nail and penny are included. Don't put the second set in the solution. This experiment make take up to 4 hours for the nail reaction to occur.

Materials

- 2 clear, plastic cups
- Plastic spoon
- 2 iron nails
- Measuring cup
- Picture and word cards for solute, solvent, solution, chemical reaction
- KWHL chart
- Safety Rules for Science Class poster
- Student Response Guide, pages 200–210
- ScienceWork, pages 70–73 and 102–103

BRING FROM HOME

Gallon of vinegar, container of salt, 2 dirty pennies

TO REPLENISH MATERIALS

Any dirty penny can be used; the nails must be iron (not coated or galvanized).

Preparation

Have the vinegar and salt ready to be mixed together.

Vocabulary

Review picture and sight word cards for this unit (see pages 189–191).

 **Engage**

STEP 1

Materials	Procedure	Follow-up
• Vinegar • Salt • 2 plastic cups • 1 iron nail • 1 dirty penny • Measuring cup • ScienceWork, pages 102–103: **What is a chemical reaction?**	Engage the students by telling them: **Today in science we're going to see how one solution can have different reactions with different materials. Let's first review how we'll know if we see a chemical reaction.** Read pages 102–103 in ScienceWork and have the students follow along. Point out that when a chemical reaction happens, they'll be able to see a change.	
	Say: **Let's begin our experiment. Here are some of our materials.** Pour ¼ cup vinegar into the measuring cup, add 1 teaspoon salt, and stir to dissolve the salt. Pour half of the solution into each cup. Show the nail and the penny to the students. Have the students examine the materials for a few moments, make comments, and ask questions.	If students ask, "What are these?" say: **Good question.**

STEP 2

Materials	Procedure	Follow-up
• 2 plastic cups with vinegar-salt solution • 1 iron nail • 1 dirty penny • Student Response Guide, page 200: **What is this?**	Hold up each material one at a time and ask: **What do you think this is? Make a guess.** Give each student a chance to guess before giving feedback. Remember, you do want students to make guesses in an inquiry lesson. Have each student respond orally with "liquid," "a solution," "a nail," or "a penny"; use an AAC device to respond; or point to responses on the Student Response Guide page. Prompt students who don't have symbol use to look at the cups and to touch the pictures in the Student Response Guide. For example, say: **You're looking at a solution. We mixed a solvent and a solute. This is a solution. Say "solution."**	Praise correct responses. If students give an incorrect answer, say: **That's a good guess.** Then give a brief reason why the choice is not the best response. For example for "clothes," say: **That's a good guess, but clothes are things you wear. Let's look again. I see a penny. This is a penny** (while pointing to the penny).

Engage

STEP 3

Materials	Procedure	Follow-up
• 1 iron nail • 1 dirty penny • 2 plastic cups with vinegar-salt solution • KWHL chart • Student Response Guide, page 201: **What do you know?**	Point to the penny and ask: **What do you know about this nail?** Have students tell something they know about the nail. Have each student respond orally, use an AAC device to respond, or point to responses on the Student Response Guide page. Prompt students who don't have symbol use to look at the nail and to touch the appropriate pictures in the Student Response Guide. For example, say: **You're looking at the metal nail. Feel it. This is metal.** Repeat the question for the penny and then the vinegar-salt solution.	Praise correct responses. Correct inappropriate responses by giving a brief reason why the response isn't the best response. For example, if "It's loud" is chosen, say: **I don't think any of the materials are loud. Look again. I think the nail is metal.** On the KWHL chart, record the correct answers in the "Know (K)" column. Draw a line to separate the responses for the nail, the penny, and the solution.

STEP 4

Materials	Procedure	Follow-up
• 1 iron nail • 1 dirty penny • KWHL chart • Student Response Guide, page 202: **What do you want to know?**	Point to the nail and the penny and ask: **What do you want to know about the nail and the penny?** Have students tell anything they might want to know about the 2 materials. Have each student respond orally, use an AAC device to respond, or point to responses on the Student Response Guide page. Prompt students who don't have symbol use to choose any picture response. Provide feedback to students to help build meaning.	Acknowledge any response. For example, if "How much do the nail and the penny cost?" is chosen, say: **That might be interesting to know.** Guide students to the answers: "Can we make the nail dirty?" and "How can we get the penny clean?" Say: **I would like to know how to make the nail dirty or maybe make the penny clean. I really want to know what will happen if we put them in the solution. How about you?** On the KWHL chart, record this response in the "Want (W)" column.

Investigate and describe relationships

STEP 5

Materials	Procedure	Follow-up
• KWHL chart • Student Response Guide, page 203: **How can we find out?**	While pointing to the "W" column on the KWHL chart, restate: **We want to know what happens if we put the nail and the penny in the solution.** Then ask: **How can we find out?** Have each student respond orally, use an AAC device to respond, or point to a response on the Student Response Guide page to say "Put them in the solution."	If students give alternate correct answers or incorrect answers, give a brief demo or explanation. For example, if they answer, "Listen to them," you might pretend to listen and say: **I don't hear anything. What else could I do?** After several students respond, acknowledge the one who answers "Put them in the solution," or point to the preferred response and say: **I think the easiest way is to put the nail and the penny in the solution.** On the KWHL chart, record responses in the "How (H)" column. Circle "Put them in the solution."

STEP 6

Materials	Procedure	Follow-up
• Plastic cups with vinegar-salt solutions • 1 iron nail • 1 dirty penny • Safety Rules for Science Class poster • Student Response Guide, page 204: **What do you think will happen?**	Review the safety rules for science listed on the poster. Then say: **Sometimes when we put a material into a solution, there is a chemical reaction. If we put the nail in one cup of solution and the penny in the other cup, do you think the nail and the penny will have the same reaction—yes or no?**	
	Have each student make a prediction by responding orally, using an AAC device to respond, pointing to a response on the Student Response Guide page, or nodding.	Tally the students' answers—how many said yes and how many said no—and record them in the open area at the bottom of the KWHL chart chart to refer to at the end of the lesson.

Investigate and describe relationships

STEP 7

Materials	Procedure	Follow-up
• Plastic cups with vinegar-salt solutions • 1 iron nail • 1 dirty penny	Say: **You each just made a prediction. Some of you said yes, the nail and the penny will both have the same reaction when they are put in the solutions, and some of you said no. Let's find out.** Instruct a student to put the nail in one of the cups. Do not submerge the nail; rather, lean it against the side of the cup so only half of the nail is in the solution. Give the nail ample time to become dirty. The exposed portion of the nail will corrode and become black. Tell another student to put the penny in the other cup. Have the other students observe. In some cases, the nail reaction may take awhile. If so, plan for the students to observe off and on throughout the day or leave overnight to observe the next day.	Describe aloud what happens, and encourage the students to tell what they see (e.g., "The penny's getting clean"). Be sure students with visual impairments actively participate in the experiment (e.g., by putting the nail or the penny in the solution).

STEP 8

Materials	Procedure	Follow-up
• 2 plastic cups with solution: 1 with the iron nail in it, the other with a dirty penny in it • Student Response Guide, page 205: **What's the same?**	Hold up the cups one at a time and say: **Here's a cup with the metal nail in the solution. Here's the other cup with the metal coin in the solution. What's the same about these 2 materials?** Have each student respond orally, use an AAC device to respond, or point to a response on the Student Response Guide page to say both cups have solutions, the nail and the penny are solids, and the nail and the penny are metal. Prompts students who don't have symbol use to look at or point to the cups.	Praise correct responses: **Yes, both cups have solutions in them, the nail and the penny are solids, and both the nail and the penny are metal.** If the students are not making a choice or are making an incorrect choice, guide them by saying, for example: **What's in both cups? Remember, we mixed the vinegar and the salt to make a solution. Is there a solution in this cup?** (Point to one of the cups.) **Is there a solution in this cup?** (Point to the other cup.) **We put solutions in both cups. That makes them the same.**

Investigate and describe relationships

Materials	Procedure	Follow-up
• 2 plastic cups with solution: 1 with the iron nail in it and the other with the dirty penny in it • Another iron nail and dirty penny • Student Response Guide, page 206: **What's different?**	Hold up the cups one at a time and say: **Let's look at the materials again. I'll take the nail out of the solution. How does it look now? Remember, this is how it looked when we put it in the solution** (show the shiny nail for comparison). **How does it look now?** Have students respond that part of the nail now looks dirty. **Now I'll take the penny out of the solution. How does it look now? Remember, this is how it looked when we put it in the solution** (show the dirty penny for comparison). **How does it look now?** Have students respond that the penny now looks clean. Tie the observations together by asking students to summarize the differences. Have each student respond orally, use an AAC device to respond, or point to a response on the Student Response Guide page to say they look different and they had different reactions.	Praise correct responses: **Yes, the nail and the penny look different, and yes, the nail and the penny had different reactions in the solution.** If the students are not making a choice or are making an incorrect choice, guide them by saying: **The nail was clean before we put it in the solution. Now it looks dirty. The penny was dirty before we put it in the solution. Now it looks clean. The nail and the penny look different. They had different chemical reactions.**

Construct explanation

STEP 10

Materials	Procedure	Follow-up
• The experimental materials • Picture and word cards for solution and chemical reaction • Student Response Guide, page 207: **What scientific discovery did we make?**	Read the scientific discovery statement once: **Solutions can cause different chemical reactions.** Say: **Let's review what we did. First we mixed the vinegar and the salt. We made a solution.** Put the picture and word cards for solution in front of either cup.	
	Give students a turn to do the same (i.e., place the picture and word cards for solution in front of either cup). Say: **Next we put the nail and the penny in the solution. The solution made them change. The nail changed to look dirtier, and the penny changed to look cleaner. The changes were chemical reactions.** Put the picture and word cards for chemical reaction in front of either cup.	Give praise: **Yes, this is solution. Say "solution."**
	Give students a turn to do the same (i.e., place the picture and word cards for chemical reaction in front of either cup). Say: **The solution changed the nail and the penny in different ways. The solution caused different chemical reactions.** For students who don't respond, prompt them to put the picture cards in front of the materials and then guide them to match the word card. Other students may be prompted to look at the materials while you or a peer places the picture and word cards. Read the scientific discovery statement again, pointing to the words on the Student Response Guide page as you read and having the students follow along.	Give praise: **Yes, this shows a chemical reaction. Say "chemical reaction."**

Report

STEP 11

Materials	Procedure	Follow-up
• The experimental materials • Picture and word cards for solution and chemical reaction • KWHL chart • Student Response Guide, pages 208–209: **What did we find out?** and **Why?**	Say: **Let's review what we found out. I asked you if you thought the chemical reactions for the nail and the penny would be the same.** Point to the predictions on the KWHL chart. **Some of you said yes, and some said no. Did putting the nail and the penny in the solutions have the same chemical reaction—yes or no?** Have each student respond orally, use an AAC device to respond, or point to a response on the Student Response Guide page, or nod yes or no.	Praise the students and then summarize: **That's correct. They did not change in the same way. The nail looks dirtier and the coin looks cleaner.** If any students respond "yes," show the before-and-after nail and penny. Write "No—the chemical reactions were different" in the open area at the bottom of the KWHL chart.
	Point to the materials and ask: **Why did the nail and the penny look different?** Have each student respond orally, use an AAC device to respond, or point to a response on the Student Response Guide page to say they had different chemical reactions. Point to the picture and words cards for chemical reaction and say: **The nail and the penny look different because solutions can cause different chemical reactions. This is the picture for solution, and this word says solution. Say "solution." This is the picture for chemical reaction and these words say chemical reaction. Say "chemical reaction."** Ask students to point to the picture and word cards for chemical reaction and solution.	Scaffold for those who don't respond by saying: **Why is one clean and one dirty?** or **Point to what made the different changes.**

Report

STEP 12		
Materials	**Procedure**	**Follow-up**
• KWHL chart • Student Response Guide, page 210: **What did we learn?**	Say: **Let's review what we learned. What can cause different chemical reactions?** Have each student respond orally with "solutions," use an AAC device to respond, or point to a response on the Student Response Guide page.	Say: **Yes, solutions can cause different chemical reactions.** Scaffold for students who say "hard" or "yellow" by asking: **What do we call the liquid?** Write "Solutions can cause different chemical reactions" in the "Learned (L)" column on the KWHL chart.

Review vocabulary

Materials: Picture and word cards for solute, solvent, solution, chemical reaction

Procedure: Use the time-delay procedure to review each of the vocabulary words for the unit. See page 8 for the procedure.

Extend and review lesson

Read the story on pages 70–71 in **ScienceWork** with the students. Help them apply the scientific concept they learned in this lesson to the story. Complete the exercise following the story together or send it home as homework.

Lesson 4 Heat and faster reactions

Concept

Solutes dissolve faster in hot solvents.

Background

In this lesson, students learn more about solvents. They learn that the temperature of solvents affects how fast solids dissolve. This lesson uses very hot water. Treat both of the solvents as you would dangerous liquids to teach students to be cautious with science materials.

Materials

- 2 measuring cups
- 2 metal spoons
- 2 thermometers capable of reading up to 212° F
- Picture and word cards for solute, solvent, solution, chemical reaction
- KWHL chart
- Safety Rules for Science Class poster
- Student Response Guide, pages 211–221
- ScienceWork, pages 74–76

BRING FROM HOME

Heat source (e.g., microwave, hot plate, electric pan, electric tea kettle), water, 3 bouillon cubes, water-soluble marker

TO REPLENISH MATERIALS

Any type of dissolvable cube will work for this experiment. The key is that the cube have color so the students can observe the cube dissolving faster in the hot water. Also note that hard, stale bouillon cubes will take longer to dissolve than soft, fresh cubes.

Preparation

Using the water-soluble marker, label the measuring cups with an A (for the hot water) and a B (for the cold water). Heat water in preparation for the experiment and pour the water into cup A to fill it about half full. The water will need to be very hot (boiling is ideal) to show a quick dissolve of the bouillion cube. Fill cup B with cold water. Place a thermometer into each cup. Prepare bouillon cubes by unwrapping them.

Vocabulary

Review picture and sight word cards for this unit (see pages 189–191).

Engage

STEP 1

Materials	Procedure	Follow-up
• 2 measuring cups with water (1 with hot, 1 with cold) and thermometers in them • 1 bouillon cube	Engage the students by telling them: **Today in science we're going to see that when we mix a solute with a solvent, the temperature of the solvent can affect how fast the solute dissolves. Here are some of our materials.**	
	Have the students examine the materials for a few moments, make comments, and ask questions.	If students ask, "What are these?" say: **Good question.**

STEP 2

Materials	Procedure	Follow-up
• 2 measuring cups with water (1 with hot, 1 with cold) and thermometers in them • 1 bouillon cube • Student Response Guide, page 211: **What is this?**	Hold up the cups of water and ask: **What do you think is in these cups? Make a guess.** Give each student a chance to guess before giving feedback. Remember, you do want students to make guesses in an inquiry lesson. Have each student respond orally with "liquid," "water," or "a solvent"; use an AAC device to respond; or point to responses on the Student Response Guide page. Prompt students who don't have symbol use to look at the cups and to touch the pictures in the Student Response Guide. For example, say: **You're looking at water.** Review the concept of solvent by saying: **This is water. Water is a solvent.** Hold up a bouillon cube and say: **I have one more material to show you. This is a bouillon cube. It's a solute.**	Praise correct responses. If students give an incorrect answer, say: **That's a good guess.** Then give a brief reason why the choice isn't the best response. For example, for "soda," say: **That's a good guess. It looks like soda, but it's actually water. Let's look again. I see water. This is water** (while pointing to the water).

Engage

STEP 3

Materials	Procedure	Follow-up
• 2 measuring cups with water (1 with hot, 1 with cold) and thermometers in them • KWHL chart • Student Response Guide, page 212: **What do you know?**	Point to the cups of water and ask: **What do you know about the water in these cups?** Have students tell something they know about the water. Have each student respond orally, use an AAC device to respond, or point to responses on the Student Response Guide page. Point out the thermometers in the cups and show how one shows the water is hot and the other shows the water is cold. Prompt students who don't have symbol use to look at the water and to touch the picture of "It's wet" in the Student Response Guide. For example, say: **You're looking at water. The water in this cup is hot. Touch hot.**	Praise correct responses. Correct inappropriate responses by giving a brief reason why the response isn't the best response. For example, if "It's cold" is chosen for the hot water cup, say: **I don't think this is cold. Look at the thermometer. It shows that the water is hot.** On the KWHL chart, record the correct answers in the "Know (K)" column. Draw a line to separate the responses for the hot water and the cold water.

STEP 4

Materials	Procedure	Follow-up
• 2 measuring cups with water (1 with hot, 1 with cold) and thermometers in them • 2 bouillon cubes • KWHL chart • Student Response Guide, page 213: **What do you want to know?**	Point to the materials and ask: **What do you want to know about these solutes and solvents?** Have students tell anything they might want to know about the materials. Have students respond orally, use their AAC devices to respond, or point to responses on the Student Response Guide page. Prompt students who don't have symbol use to choose any picture response. Provide feedback to students to help build meaning.	Acknowledge any response. For example, if "Will the reactions make noise?" is chosen, say: **That would be interesting to find out.** Guide students to the answer: "What temperature will create a faster reaction?" Say: **I would like to know what temperature will create a faster reaction. How about you?** On the KWHL chart, record this response in the "Want (W)" column.

Investigate and describe relationships

STEP 5

Materials	Procedure	Follow-up
• KWHL chart • Student Response Guide, page 214: **How can we find out?**	While pointing to the "W" column on the KWHL chart, restate: **We want to know what temperature will create a faster reaction.** Then ask: **How can we find out?** Have each student respond orally, use an AAC device to respond, point to a response on the Student Response Guide page, or pantomime a stirring action.	If students give alternate correct answers or incorrect answers, give a brief demo or explanation. For example, if they answer "Look at them," let them look at the cups and say: **That didn't give us much information. What else could we do?** After several students respond, acknowledge the one who answers "Drop them in hot and cold water," or point to the preferred response and say: **I think the easiest way to find out is to drop the cubes in hot and cold water.** On the KWHL chart, record responses in the "How (H)" column. Circle "Drop them in hot and cold water."

Investigate and describe relationships

STEP 6

Materials	Procedure	Follow-up
• 2 measuring cups with water (1 with hot, 1 with cold) and thermometers in them • 2 bouillon cubes • KWHL chart • Safety Rules for Science Class poster • Student Response Guide, page 215: **What do you think will happen?**	Review the safety rules for science on the poster. Put a bouillon cube in front of each cup of water to show students what will be mixed. Say: **We're going to put a bouillon cube into each cup and see what happens when we stir them. The water is the solvent, and the cubes are the solute. The temperature of the water in cup A is very hot** (point to the thermometer), **and the water in cup B is cold** (point to the thermometer). **Different things may happen to the solute when the solvent is hot versus when it is cold. Which cup of water do you think will dissolve the cube faster—cup A with hot water or cup B with cold water?** Point to the cups.	
	Have each student make a prediction by responding orally, using an AAC device to respond, pointing to a response on the Student Response Page, or nodding when you say "hot" or "cold."	Tally the students' answers—how many said hot and how many said cold—and record them in the open area at the bottom of the KWHL chart to refer to at the end of the lesson.

Investigate and describe relationships

STEP 7		
Materials	**Procedure**	**Follow-up**
• 2 measuring cups with water (1 with hot, 1 with cold) and thermometers in them • 2 bouillon cubes • 2 metal spoons	Say: **You each just made a prediction. Some of you said the cube will dissolve faster in the hot water, and some said cold water. Let's find out.** Make certain the water in cup A is still boiling hot. If not, reheat it. Have one student put the cube into cup A and another student stir. Have another student put the cube into cup B and another student stir. Remind students that when a solute (the cube) is mixed with a solvent (the water), they'll create a solution. Have students stir until the cube in cup A is dissolved. Remove the cube from cup B (because of the cold water the cube should still be partially in cube form) to illustrate to students that the cold water did not fully dissolve the cube.	Describe aloud what happens. For example, say: **The cube in cup A is dissolving. We can tell because the water is changing colors. The cube in cup B still looks like a cube. We're still stirring.** Encourage the students to tell what they see (e.g., "The water is brown"). Be sure students with visual impairments actively participate in the experiment (e.g., by stirring the mixture or by hearing you describe what is happening). Another idea to emphasize the time difference is to have one student sound a buzzer or hit a switch when the solute is completely dissolved in a given cup.

Investigate and describe relationships

STEP 8

Materials	Procedure	Follow-up
• Measuring cups A and B and the partially dissolved cube • Student Response Guide, page 216: **What's the same?**	Point to the cups one at a time and say: **Here's cup A, with the hot water and the cube dissolved. Here is cup B, with the cold water, and here's the cube partly dissolved. Remember, when we mix a solute** (point to the cube) **and a solvent** (point to the water) **we get a solution. What's the same about what's in cups A and B?** Have each student respond orally, use an AAC device to respond, or point to a response on the Student Response Guide page to say they are both solutions. Prompt students who don't have symbol use to look at or touch a cup after another student correctly identifies they are both solutions.	Praise correct responses: **Yes, they are both solutions. That makes them the same.** If the students are not making a choice or are making an incorrect choice, hold up one cup at a time and say: **Look at cup A. Remember we added the cube—the solute—to the hot water—the solvent. Then we added another cube—the solute—to the cold water—the solvent—in cup B. A solute + a solvent = a solution. These are both solutions. That makes them the same.**

STEP 9

Materials	Procedure	Follow-up
• Measuring cups A and B and the partially dissolved cube • Student Response Guide, page 217: **What's different?**	Hold up the cups one at a time and say: **Here's cup A, with the hot water and the cube dissolved. Here's cup B, with the cold water, and here's the cube partly dissolved. What's different about how cups A and B dissolved the cube?** Have each student respond orally, use an AAC device to respond, or point to a response on the Student Response Guide page to say one dissolved faster. Prompt students who don't have symbol use to look at or touch the cup that the cube dissolved in faster.	Praise correct responses: **Yes, one dissolved the cube fast, and the other was slow.** If the students are not making a choice or are making an incorrect choice, hold up one cup at a time and say: **Let's look at both of the cups. When we put the cube in the cup of hot water, the cube started to dissolve very fast. The cube isn't in the cup anymore. It dissolved. When we put the cube in the cup of cold water, the cube dissolved slowly. The cube didn't finish dissolving** (point to the partially dissolved cube in front of cup B). **The cubes dissolved at different speeds. One was fast and one was slow.**

Construct explanation

Materials	Procedure	Follow-up
• 1 bouillon cube • Measuring cups A and B and the partially dissolved cube • Picture and word cards for solute, solvent, solution • Student Response Guide, page 218: **What scientific discovery did we make?**	Read the scientific discovery statement once: **Solutes dissolve faster in hot solvents.** Say: **Let's review what we did. First we had cubes. The cubes are solutes.** Put the picture and word cards for solute in front of the bouillon cube.	
	Give students a turn to do the same (i.e., put the picture and word cards in front of the cube). For students who don't respond, have them put the picture cards with the cube and then guide them to match the word card. Other students may be prompted to look at the cube while you or a peer places the picture and word cards. **Next we had cups with hot and cold water. Those were the solvents.** Put the picture and word cards for solvent in front of the cups of water.	Give praise: **Yes, this is the cube. It is a solute.**
	Give students a turn to do the same (i.e., put the picture and word cards in front of the cups of water).	Give praise: **Yes, this is the solvent.**

(Step continues)

Construct explanation

Materials	Procedure	Follow-up
	Then we mixed the solute (point to the cube) **and the solvent** (point to the cup of water) **to create a solution. We watched to see if the cubes would dissolve faster in the hot solvent or in the cold solvent. Here are the solutions we made.** Put the picture and word cards for solution in front of cup A.	
	Give students a turn to do the same (i.e., put the picture and word cards in front of cup A). For students who don't respond, have them put the picture cards in front of the cube and then guide them to match the word card. Other students may be prompted to look at the cube while you or a peer places the picture and word cards. Read the scientific discovery statement again, pointing to the words on the Student Response Guide page as you read and having the students follow along.	Give praise: **Yes, this is the solution.**

Report

STEP 11		
Materials	**Procedure**	**Follow-up**
• Measuring cups A and B and the partially dissolved cube • Picture and word cards for solvent • KWHL chart • Student Response Guide, pages 219–220: **What did we find out?** and **Why?**	Say: **Let's review what we found out. I asked you if you thought the cube would dissolve faster in the hot water or the cold water?** Point to the predictions on the KWHL chart. **Some of you said hot, and some said cold. In which cup of water did the cube dissolve faster— the one with the hot water or the one with the cold water?** Have each student respond orally, use an AAC device to respond, point to a response on the Student Response Guide page, or nod yes or no when you say "hot" or "cold."	Praise the students and then summarize: **Good, the cube dissolved faster in the hot solvent. The cube started to dissolve in the cold solvent, but it took a long time.** If any students respond "cold," point to cup A and the thermometer. Remind them that the cube dissolved fast. Write "hot solvent" in the open area at the bottom of the KWHL chart.
	Point to cup A and say: **Why did the cube dissolve faster in cup A?** Have each student respond orally, use an AAC device to respond, or point to a response on the Student Response Guide page to indicate that the solvent was hot. Ask students to point to the picture and word cards for solvent.	Point to cup A and say: **We put the solutes in solvents that were different temperatures. The solutes dissolved at different speeds. One dissolved quickly because the solvent was hot.** Scaffold for those who don't respond by asking: **What temperature was the solvent in cup A?**

Report

STEP 12

Materials	Procedure	Follow-up
• Measuring cups A and B and the partially dissolved cube • KWHL chart • Student Response Guide, page 221: **What did we learn?**	Say: **Let's review what we learned. What kind of solvent helps a solute dissolve faster? Solutes dissolve faster in _____ solvents.** Have each student respond orally with "hot," use an AAC device to respond, or point to a response on the Student Response Guide page to fill in the blank.	Say: **Yes, a hot solvent will dissolve a solute faster.** Scaffold for students who say "cold," by rephrasing the question: **How does this cup feel? It's hot.** Write "Solutes dissolve faster in hot solvents" in the "Learned (L)" column of the KWHL chart.

Review vocabulary

Materials: Picture and word cards for solute, solvent, solution, chemical reaction

Procedure: Use the time-delay procedure to review each of the vocabulary words for the unit. See page 8 for the procedure.

Extend and review lesson

Read the story on page 74 in **ScienceWork** with the students. Help them apply the scientific concept they learned in this lesson to the story. Complete the exercise following the story together or send it home as homework.

Lesson 5 Helpful and harmful solutions

Concept

Some chemical solutions are harmful. Some chemical solutions are helpful.

Background

In this lesson, students learn more about chemical solutions. They learn that some chemical solutions are helpful to living things, while others are harmful. For safety, this lesson uses bleach water and plant food as the chemical solutions. Treat the solutions as you would dangerous chemicals to teach students to be cautious with all chemicals and materials. Note that this experiment extends over a 2-week time period.

Materials

- 2 spray bottles
- Plant food
- Picture and word cards for solute, solvent, solution, chemical reaction
- KWHL chart
- Safety Rules for Science Class poster
- Student Response Guide, pages 222–232
- ScienceWork, pages 77–79 and 104

BRING FROM HOME

Container of bleach and 2 live plants (as similar as possible; oftentimes inexpensive prepotted plants [like basil or herbs] can be bought in the produce section of grocery stores), permanent marker, water

TO REPLENISH MATERIALS

Replenish plant food as needed; liquid or powder will work. If needed, spray bottles are inexpensive to purchase at dollar stores.

Preparation

Using a permanent marker, write the number 1 on one spray bottle and on the container of one plant. Put approximately ¼ cup of bleach in the bottle, then fill with water. Write the number 2 on the second spray bottle and on the second plant. Add water and the plant food as directed on the package of plant food to spray bottle 2. Have the bleach and plant food package available for students to examine.

Vocabulary

Review picture and sight word cards for this unit (see pages 189–191).

 *Engage*

STEP 1		
Materials	**Procedure**	**Follow-up**
• Spray bottles 1 and 2 with solutions in them • Bleach bottle • Package of plant food	Engage the students by telling them: **Today in science we're going to see that some solutions in our daily lives can be helpful and some can be harmful.**	
	Open the spray bottles so students are able to see the consistency and color of the contents. Show the packages (of bleach and plant food) to the students and invite them to examine them for a few moments, make comments, and ask questions.	If students ask, "What are these?" say: **Good question.**

 Engage

STEP 2		
Materials	**Procedure**	**Follow-up**
• Spray bottles 1 and 2 with solutions in them • Bleach bottle • Package of plant food • Student Response Guide, page 222: **What is this?**	Hold up the spray bottles one at a time and ask: **What do you think is in this bottle? Make a guess.** Give each student a chance to guess before giving feedback. Remember, you do want students to make guesses in an inquiry lesson. Hold up the package of plant food or the bottle of bleach to help in the guessing process. Have each student respond orally with "bleach," "solution," or "plant food"; use an AAC device to respond; or point to responses on the Student Response Guide page. Prompt students who don't have symbol use to look at the package of plant food or the bottle of bleach and touch the pictures in the Student Response Guide. For example, say: **You're looking at bleach. This is bleach.** Review the concept of solution. While holding the spray bottles, say: **This is bleach solution. I mixed bleach into a water solvent to make this bleach solution. And this is a plant food solution. I mixed plant food into a water solvent to make this plant food solution. These bottles both have liquids in them, and these liquids will be the chemical solutions we'll use in our experiment today.**	Praise correct responses. If students give an incorrect answer, say: **That's a good guess.** Then give a brief reason why the choice isn't the best response. For example for "milk," say: **That's a good guess. It looks a bit like milk, but it's actually bleach. This is plant food, and this is bleach. They're both liquids. They're both chemical solutions.**

 Engage

STEP 3

Materials	Procedure	Follow-up
• Spray bottles 1 and 2 with solutions in them • KWHL chart • Student Response Guide, page 223: **What do you know?**	Point to spray bottle 1 and ask: **What do you know about what's in this spray bottle?** Have the students tell something they know about the solution. Have each student respond orally, use an AAC device to respond, or point to responses on the Student Response Guide page. Prompt students who don't have symbol use to look at the bleach bottle or the plant food container and to touch the picture of "It's wet" in the Student Response Guide. For example, say: **You're looking at bleach solution. It is a liquid and it's wet.** Repeat the question for spray bottle 2.	Praise correct responses. Correct inappropriate answers by giving a brief reason why the response isn't the best response. For example, if "It's dry" is chosen, say: **I don't think it's dry. Look at it move in the bottle. This is a liquid.** On the KWHL chart, record the correct answers in the "Know (K)" column.

STEP 4

Materials	Procedure	Follow-up
• 2 live plants • Spray bottles 1 and 2 with solutions in them • KWHL chart • Student Response Guide, page 224: **What do you want to know?**	Show the live plants to the students. Point to the plants and the spray bottles and ask: **What do you want to know about the plants and the solutions?** Have students tell anything they might want to know about the materials. Have students respond orally, use their AAC devices to respond, or point to responses on the Student Response Guide page. Prompt students who don't have symbol use to choose any picture response. Provide feedback to students to help build meaning.	Acknowledge any response. For example, if "Will the plants flower? is chosen, say: **That would be interesting. It's easy to tell the plants won't flower because there are no flower buds.** Guide students to the answer: "Will the plants grow with chemical solutions sprayed on them?" Say: **I would like to know if the plants will grow if I spray these chemical solutions on them. How about you?** On the KWHL chart, record this response in the "Want (W)" column.

Investigate and describe relationships

STEP 5

Materials	Procedure	Follow-up
• KWHL chart • Student Response Guide, page 225: **How can we find out?**	While pointing to the "W" column on the KWHL chart, restate: **We want to know if the plants will grow when we spray these chemical solutions on them.** Then ask: **How can we find out?** Have each student respond orally, use an AAC device to respond, point to a response on the Student Response Guide page, or pantomime a spraying action.	If students give alternate correct answers or incorrect answers, give a brief demo or explanation. For example, if they answer "Talk to them," let them talk to the plants and say: **That didn't give us much information. What else could we do?** After several students respond, acknowledge the one who answers "Spray the plants with the solutions," or point to the preferred response and say: **I think the easiest way to find out is to spray the solutions on them.** On the KWHL chart, record responses in the "How (H)" column. Circle "Spray the plants with the solutions."

Investigate and describe relationships

STEP 6

Materials	Procedure	Follow-up
• 2 live plants • Spray bottles 1 and 2 with solutions in them • Safety Rules for Science Class poster • Student Response Guide, page 226: **What do you think will happen?**	Review the safety rules for science listed on the poster. Say: **I put bleach into water and then put the solution in bottle 1** (point to bottle 1). **Then I put plant food into water in bottle 2** (point to bottle 2). **Now we'll spray plant 1 with the chemical solution in bottle 1** (point to bottle 1), **and spray plant 2 with the chemical solution in bottle 2** (point to bottle 2). **Plants are livings things and will grow if we take care of them. We'll watch our plants every day for 2 weeks to see what happens when we spray them with the chemical solutions. We'll find out if the chemical solutions are helpful to the plants. Remember, the chemicals we're using are already mixed. They are chemical solutions. Which chemical solution do you think will be helpful to the plants? Which solution will help the plants grow—solution 1 with the bleach or solution 2 with the plant food?**	
	Have each student make a prediction by responding orally, using an AAC device to respond, pointing to a response on the Student Response Page, or nodding when you say "solution 1" or "solution 2?"	Tally the students' answers—how many said solution 1 and how many said solution 2—and record them in the open area at the bottom of the KWHL chart to refer to at the end of the lesson.

Investigate and describe relationships

STEP 7

Materials	Procedure	Follow-up
• 2 live plants • Spray bottles 1 and 2 with solutions in them • ScienceWork, page 104: **Observation of the plants** chart	Say: **You each just made a prediction. Some of you said solution 1 will help the plant, and some said solution 2 will help the plants. We'll find out, but this experiment will take a little longer than our others. Let's get started.** Before beginning, help students observe how the plants look at the start of the experiment and make notes in their ScienceWorks **Observation of the plants** chart. Have one student spray plant 1 with solution 1. Repeat for plant 2. Say: **Each day for the next 2 weeks, we're going to spray the plants with the chemicals and keep track of how they look on the observations chart.** Repeat spraying, observing, and charting for 2 weeks or until a visible difference in plant 1 versus plant 2 is observed.	Describe aloud what is observed, and encourage the students to tell what they see (e.g., "The leaves are turning yellow," or "The plant is growing"). Be sure students with visual impairments actively participate in the experiment (e.g., by spraying the solution or by touching the plants to feel a difference in the leaves).

Investigate and describe relationships

STEP 8

Materials	Procedure	Follow-up
• Plants 1 and 2 • Spray bottles 1 and 2 • ScienceWork, page 104: **Observation of the plants** chart • Student Response Guide, page 227: **What's the same?**	Hold up the plants one at a time and say: **Here is plant 1. Here is plant 2. For the past couple of weeks, we've sprayed the plants with a chemical solution. Let's look at your observation charts, and let's look at the plants. What's the same about these two materials?** Have each student respond orally, use an AAC device to respond, or point to a response on the Student Response Guide page to say both are plants. Prompt students who don't have symbol use to look at or touch the plants after another student correctly identifies that both are plants. Repeat the question for the spray bottles with the solutions.	Praise correct responses: **Yes, they're both plants. That makes them the same.** If the students are not making a choice or are making an incorrect choice, hold up each plant and say: **What is this? Yes, this is a plant. And what is this? Yes, this is a plant too. Both are plants, and that makes them the same. Repeat these questions for the chemical solutions in the spray bottles if needed.**

Construct explanation

STEP 9

Materials	Procedure	Follow-up
• Plants 1 and 2 • Spray bottles 1 and 2 • Student Response Guide, page 228: **What's different?**	Hold up the plants one at a time and say: **Here's plant 1. Here is plant 2. For the past couple of weeks, we've sprayed the plants with a chemical solution. What's different about these plants?** Have each student respond orally, use an AAC device to respond, or point to a response on the Student Response Guide page to say the plants look different. Hold up the spray bottles one at a time and say: **Remember, when we started we had a bleach water solution in bottle 1 and a plant food solution in bottle 2. What's different about these materials?** Have each student respond orally, use an AAC device to respond, or point to a response on the Student Response Guide page to say they're different chemical solutions. Prompt students who don't have symbol use to look at or touch the plants after another student answers.	Praise correct responses: **Yes, the plants look different. One is healthy and has grown. The other has wilted leaves and looks like it's dying. The chemical solutions we used were different.** If the students are not making a choice or are making an incorrect choice, hold up the plants and say: **Let's look at both plants. We sprayed chemical solution 1—the bleach solution—on plant 1. It wilted and died. We sprayed chemical solution 2—the plant food—on plant 2. It grew and stayed healthy. Chemical solution 1 was harmful. Chemical solution 2 was helpful to the plant.**

Construct explanation

STEP 10

Materials	Procedure	Follow-up
• Plants 1 and 2 • Spray bottles 1 and 2 • Picture and word cards for solution • Student Response Guide, page 229: **What scientific discovery did we make?**	Read the scientific discovery statement once: **Some chemical solutions are harmful. Some chemical solutions are helpful.** Say: **Let's review what we did. First I made different chemical solutions and put one in spray bottle 1 and the other in spray bottle 2. Then we sprayed the chemical solutions on the plants. We watched and charted the plants every day to see what the chemical solutions did to the plants.** Put the picture and word cards for solution in front of the spray bottles.	
	Give students a turn to do the same (i.e., put the picture and word cards in front of the spray bottles). For students who don't respond, have them put the picture cards with the spray bottles and then guide them to match the word card. Other students may be prompted to look at the spray bottles while you or a peer places the picture and word cards. Read the scientific discovery statement again, pointing to the words on the Student Response Guide page as you read and having the students follow along.	Give praise: **Good. Both of the bottles had a chemical solution in them, but they were different chemical solutions. We sprayed both plants with chemical solutions, but only bottle 2 had a helpful chemical solution in it.** Say "solution."

Report

STEP 11

Materials	Procedure	Follow-up
• Plants 1 and 2 • Picture and word cards for solution • KWHL chart • Student Response Guide, pages 230–231: **What did we find out?** and **Why?**	Say: **Let's review what we found out. I asked you which chemical solution you thought would be helpful to the plants—which solution would help them grow.** Point to the predictions on the KWHL chart. **Some of you said solution 1** (point to spray bottle 1), **and some said solution 2** (point to spray bottle 2). **Which chemical solution was helpful to the plants—solution 1 or solution 2?** Have each student respond orally, use an AAC device to respond, or point to a response on the Student Response Guide page, or nod yes or no when you say "solution 1" or "solution 2."	Praise the students and then summarize: **Good, the chemical solution in bottle 2 was helpful to the plant.** If any students respond "solution 1," show the dead plant and ask if the solution was helpful or harmful. Write "solution 2—helpful; solution 1—harmful" in the open area at the bottom of the KWHL chart.
	Point to plant 2 and ask: **Why did plant 2 grow?** Have each student respond orally, use an AAC device to respond, or point to a response on the Student Response Guide page to indicate that chemical solution 2 was helpful. Ask students to point to the picture and word cards for solution.	Point to plant 2 and say: **Yes, solution 2 was a helpful solution, and solution 1 was harmful.** Scaffold for those who don't respond by reminding students: **Some chemical solutions are harmful and some chemical solutions are helpful.**

Report

STEP 12

Materials	Procedure	Follow-up
• KWHL chart • Student Response Guide, page 232: **What did we learn?**	Say: **We learned what happened to the plants with helpful and harmful chemical solutions. Remember, plants are living things. What can chemical solutions do to living things? Some chemical solutions _____ living things. Some chemical solutions _____ living things.** Have each student respond orally with "harm" and "help," use an AAC device to respond, or point to responses on the Student Response Guide page to fill in the blanks.	Scaffold for students who say "laugh at" by rephrasing the question: **What did we say the chemical solutions did to the plants?** Write "Some chemical solutions are harmful. Some chemical solutions are helpful" in the "Learned (L)" column of the KWHL chart.

Review vocabulary

Materials: Picture and word cards for solute, solvent, solution, chemical reaction

Procedure: Use the time-delay procedure to review each of the vocabulary words for the unit. See page 8 for the procedure.

Extend and review lesson

Read the story on page 77 in **ScienceWork** with the students. Help them apply the scientific concept they learned in this lesson to the story. Complete the exercise following the story together or send it home as homework.

Research findings

INTRODUCTION

Teaching skills to students with moderate and severe developmental disabilities linked to their state's grade-level content standards is an innovation that was fostered by recent legislation, including the No Child Left Behind Act (NCLB, 2002) and the Individuals with Disabilities Education Act (IDEA, 2004). For the first time, schools are accountable for all students making adequate yearly progress in language arts, mathematics, and science content standards. For students with significant cognitive disabilities, this progress could be based on alternate achievement of their state's standards in these academic areas. Although reauthorization of these major education acts often creates changes, what is most likely to persist is the educational opportunity to learn academic content that is appropriate to students' chronological age and grade. **Teaching to Standards: Math** and **Teaching to Standards: Science** were created to provide examples of how to make grade-level content for students with moderate and severe developmental disabilities both accessible and achievable. The target is alternate achievement of content that has been streamlined and prioritized. Students learn grade-level content but with alternate achievement.

Teaching to Standards: Math and **Teaching to Standards: Science** were developed based on comprehensive reviews of the research literature and then evaluated in applications by teachers in programs for students with developmental disabilities, including intellectual disabilities and autism. In a comprehensive review of mathematics, Browder, Spooner, Ahlgrim-Delzell, Wakeman, and Harris (2008)

found 68 studies of individuals with moderate and severe developmental disabilities. Most studies focused on numbers and operations or money management, but a few focused on the other strands of mathematics (e.g., geometry) identified by the National Council of Teachers of Mathematics (2000). Based on this review, we identified task analytic instruction with systematic prompting as being an evidence-based procedure for teaching specific mathematics skills. In a task analysis, the teacher provides step-by-step instructions on a chain of responses to complete the activity. In the case of math activities, this would be the steps to complete a math problem. By using guidelines from the National Science Education Standards (National Research Council, 1996) to identify science content, Courtade, Spooner, and Browder (2007) found 11 studies that had some intersect with science. Their review also revealed the importance of systematic prompting and feedback, but also the need for new methods that could be used to teach scientific inquiry.

We chose to focus on upper-level mathematics and science content because this can be especially challenging to adapt for students who begin with little background to understand this material. We decided to design examples of content in several areas of science and mathematics to illustrate how adaptations could be made across curricular areas. For each type of learning, we researched current thinking within general education about how to teach these content areas. For mathematics, we used a literacy-based approach in which the math problem was embedded in a simple story. Literature in mathematics education suggests that stories can provide a schema for students to organize facts

(Anderson, Spiro, & Anderson, 1978; Zambo, 2005). We also had experienced some success in using read-alouds of middle school literature as a means to teach grade-linked content in language arts (Browder, Trela, & Jimenez, 2007) and in using task analysis to teach the steps to solve a problem (Jimenez, Browder, & Courtade, 2008). For science, we chose an inquiry-based approach based on recommendations of the National Research Council (NRC, 1996). Because the field of science is ever-changing and expanding, inquiry-based instruction teaches students to be active participants in the world that is changing around them. Courtade, Browder, Spooner, and DiBiase (2008) provided some preliminary evidence that teachers are able to implement inquiry-based lessons, so that students can gain increased independence in participation in these lessons.

In the 2006–07 school year, we implemented the literacy-based approach to mathematics and inquiry-based approach to science with students in the Charlotte-Mecklenburg School System (NC) through funding received from the U.S. Department of Education Office of Special Education Programs (Grant No. H324M03003). The following briefly summarizes the method we used and results obtained. A full report of this research can be obtained from Diane Browder at the University of North Carolina at Charlotte. The opinions expressed here do not necessarily reflect the position or policy of the Department of Education, and no official endorsement should be inferred.

METHOD

Participants and setting

We recruited 10 middle and high school special education teachers for this research. Teachers were randomly assigned to receive either the math or science lesson model plans. Depending on their assignment, special education teachers then invited either a math or science general education teacher as a collaborative partner.

While the teachers could implement the model lessons with all of their students, 2–3 students in their class served as participants in this research. We obtained informed consent to observe and assess these target students. There were a total of 42 student participants, including 11 students with autism and 31 with moderate intellectual disabilities. To be eligible, students had to have a full-scale IQ below 55. The model lessons were taught in the students' special education classrooms. During the teacher training days, the general and special education teachers were given time to plan inclusive activities as well as to review the content of the lessons. Only a few students had opportunities to participate in the general education classes, and no research data were taken in these contexts.

Math and science model lessons

The model lessons were those that are now available in **Teaching to the Standards: Math** and **Teaching to the Standards: Science.** Math skills included solving an algebraic equation, graphing (data analysis), identifying points on a plane (geometry), and computing the next dollar amount. Science included Earth's waters, Earth's history, chemistry, and microbiology. These specific skills were chosen in consultation with general education curriculum experts as ones that would be pivotal to the overall content standards. In math, teachers received stories for teaching each math concept, the graphic organizers needed to complete the response (e.g., the "equation prompt" in algebra), and the written lesson plans. In science, the teachers received the materials needed to conduct the experiment, science vocabulary flashcards, the written lesson plans, and student response boards.

Measurement of the dependent variables

The dependent variables for this research were a Math Assessment and a Science Assessment created by the research team. All assessments were implemented by members of the research team. In math, a task analysis was created for each of the skills in the various domains (e.g., geometry, data analysis). These assessments are now available in **Teaching to Standards: Math.** To assess the student, the teacher presented any necessary math manipulatives and the graphic organizer, then asked the student to perform the math problem (e.g., create the graph, find the points on a plane). Each skill was scored as either independently correct or incorrect. No prompts or feedback were given during testing. In science, a task analysis for participation in an inquiry lesson was created. One of the researchers implemented an inquiry-based lesson with the research participants in a small group. The researcher scored the student's participation as independently correct or incorrect. The researcher then tested each student alone on identification of the science vocabulary. This test required making three responses for each vocabulary word: (1) reading the word (no picture), (2) identifying the picture (without the printed word), and (3) matching the word to the picture (to show comprehension). A total of 20 vocabulary words were presented that related to each of the science units.

Research design

The research design was a group quasi-experimental design with students serving as the unit of analysis. Teachers were randomly assigned to receive training in either the mathematics or science intervention. Because the interventions were highly dissimilar and teachers received only one of the two sets of model plans, it was hypothesized that there would be no treatment interference. Teachers continued their ongoing instruction in the content area not chosen for the model plans. For example, in mathematics, most teachers focused on teaching students to identify and count money. In science, teachers used discussions of an online news magazine. While most teachers instructed students on money skills

daily, science lessons in the control condition were sporadic.

Teacher training

After being assigned to receive either the model math or model science lessons, the teachers attended workshops with their math or science general education teacher partner, depending on the assigned content. At each workshop, the teachers received some background information on the particular domain of content (e.g., algebra or Earth's history), discussed state standards and general education priorities in this content, viewed videotape demonstrations from a pilot year, and then learned to implement the specific target lessons through role-play practice. Following the training, teachers implemented one domain of content between each workshop. For example, after the first math workshop, the teachers received and implemented the lesson plans for algebra. Two months later, they received and implemented geometry. Similarly, the teachers received the science units one at a time.

RESULTS

Interrater reliability

A second researcher observed and scored 40% of all tests administered. Interrater reliability was computed as agreements over total responses scored and was 99% for these observations.

Mathematics achievement

As shown in Tables 1 and 2, strong effects for mathematics were found for the differences between the treatment and control group across all math units. An analysis of variance revealed significant differences for the interaction effects in geometry, algebra, and measurement and across all units. A significant effect was not found for data analysis. This finding may have been influenced by the small sample size and the treatment group's higher pretest scores.

Table 1: Effect Size for Math Unit Assessments

	Pretest		Posttest		
	M	*SD*	*M*	*SD*	Cohen *d*
Geometry					
Control	3.19	1.99	3.95	2.43	
Treatment	3.88	2.49	7.06	2.27	1.29
Algebra					
Control	3.14	1.35	0.14	0.35	
Treatment	3.29	1.89	4.00	4.37	1.70
Data Analysis					
Control	2.14	3.00	2.81	3.66	
Treatment	4.59	3.79	6.35	3.08	1.01
Measurement					
Control	0.52	0.60	0.14	0.35	
Treatment	0.76	0.66	4.00	4.37	1.29
Total Score					
Control	9.00	5.18	10.48	6.73	
Treatment	12.53	6.80	24.18	10.03	1.60

Table 2: ANOVA for Math Unit Assessments

	Outcome Effect		*F-Ratio*	n^2_p
Geometry	Within Ss	Pre/Post	41.54**	0.54
		Interaction	15.61**	0.30
	Between Ss	Instruction	7.67**	0.17
Algebra	Within Ss	Pre/Post	7.56**	0.17
		Interaction	19.72**	0.35
	Between Ss	Instruction	9.53**	0.21
Data Analysis	Within Ss	Pre/Post	6.99*	0.16
		Interaction	1.43	0.03
	Between Ss	Instruction	8.80**	0.19
Measurement	Within Ss	Pre/Post	9.06**	0.20
		Interaction	14.55**	0.28
	Between Ss	Instruction	16.62**	0.32
All Units	Within Ss	Pre/Post	69.41**	0.66
		Interaction	41.70**	0.54
	Between Ss	Instruction	14.87**	0.30

Note: Degrees of freedom for all tests of significance was 1,37.

$*p < .05.$ $**p < .01.$

SCIENCE ACHIEVEMENT

In science, differences between the treatment and control were found for the acquisition of science vocabulary, but not for participation in the inquiry lesson (see Tables 3 and 4). The treatment group had strong effects for acquisition of the science vocabulary. The interaction between treatment and control group showed a significant difference for vocabulary on the analysis of variance. In contrast, the control group, who received the math intervention, also showed an increase on the posttest in scientific inquiry. Differences between groups in inquiry were not significant. While the reason for the control group's growth is unknown, it is hypothesized that the training in mathematical problem solving generalized to lessons in scientific inquiry. An alternative explanation is that the math intervention increased students' active participation in academic learning, which generalized to the science inquiry activity.

Table 3: Effect Size for Vocabulary and Inquiry Assessments

	Pretest		Posttest		
	M	SD	M	SD	Cohen d
Vocabulary					
Control	22.89	7.91	23.44	9.34	0.06
Treatment	22.95	7.95	32.62	13.77	0.86
Inquiry					
Control	9.44	2.43	11.39	2.95	0.72
Treatment	8.48	2.29	11.62	3.04	1.17

Table 4: ANOVA for Vocabulary and Inquiry Assessments

	Outcome Effect		F-Ratio	n^2_p
Vocabulary	Within Ss	Pre/Post	11.79**	0.24
		Interaction	9.36**	0.20
	Between Ss	Instruction	2.55	0.06
Inquiry	Within Ss	Pre/Post	44.73**	0.55
		Interaction	2.48	0.06
	Between Ss	Instruction	.22	<0.01

Note: Degrees of freedom for all tests of significance was 1,37.
**$p < .01$.

DISCUSSION AND IMPLICATIONS FOR PRACTICE

For a practice to be considered evidence-based, the design of the experiment should minimize threats to internal and external validity and the intervention should be replicated with new groups of students. The model mathematics and science lessons used in **Teaching to Standards: Math** and **Teaching to Standards: Science** should be considered a promising practice because of the initial evidence found for student learning in a quasi-experimental design. Teachers are encouraged to conduct their own student assessments to determine if this intervention is effective for individual learners. In contrast, while this is the first study to evaluate the Teaching to Standards materials, the lesson plans were based on comprehensive reviews of research by

Browder et al. (2008) and Courtade, Spooner, and Browder (2007) and well-established methods for students with moderate and severe developmental disabilities, including task analytic instruction and systematic instruction with feedback.

To achieve positive outcomes with students, it is recommended that the instructional guidelines are followed and then individual modifications are made as needed. For example, the math lesson plans have been developed to follow a most-to-least intrusive prompting system (Collins, 2007). In the early lessons, teachers provide a model so that students can learn the math procedures with minimal errors. Over lessons, the teacher provides progressively less assistance for each step of the task analysis. By the last lesson, the student performs the math procedure while the teacher observes. Although not all students may achieve this level of independence, through systematic instruction and fading of prompts, students are more likely to learn the steps of the task analysis.

In science, the inquiry process requires allowing students to make some guesses. This may be new for teachers who are used to using errorless learning procedures. By following the lesson guidelines, the teacher can provide students the opportunity to make observations and form hypotheses with structure and support so that the target concept is learned. In contrast, when teaching the vocabulary, an errorless learning procedure called *time delay* is recommended (Collins, 2007). Rapid review of the science flashcards with a model gives the student the opportunity to practice naming words that may be new vocabulary. Then through a brief time delay, the teacher waits for the student to anticipate correct answers on known words. All of the guidelines provide help for praising correct responses and correcting any student mistakes. This feedback is also key to student success.

In our research, the opportunities for students to learn the material or practice the skills in inclusive settings occurred only sporadically. When teaching these skills in a general education class, it will be important to select the lessons that match the focus of the class. These lessons may provide additional practice for students who are nondisabled who might serve as peer tutors. In science, teaching students to follow the steps of inquiry and use the KWHL chart may be skills that will transfer across the rapidly changing content of the general education class.

Some students with developmental disabilities do not yet use symbols to communicate independently. We recommend using the symbols in these lessons with all students to give them the opportunity to gain meaning from symbols. In contrast, the goal for student learning may be more concrete for some students. For example, some students in math may be able to create a graph using small objects independently, but need assistance to complete the student worksheet. In science, some students may learn a subset of the inquiry responses. For example, a student may be able to perform the experiment or indicate which of two items is different even if they need assistance to then summarize their findings using the student response pictures.

In conclusion, this early research suggests that Teaching to Standards may be a promising practice for teaching grade-level content with alternate achievement. Multiple studies are needed to confirm an intervention to be evidence-based. This promising practice was derived from comprehensive reviews of the research literature on teaching math and science to students with moderate and severe disabilities. By following the research-based guidelines including the step-by-step (task analyzed) lessons with the systematic prompting and feedback, teachers are more likely to promote student success. Ongoing student assessments are important to determine if this intervention works for individual students.

Name _____

KWHL chart

What do you **K**now?	What do you **W**ant to know?	**H**ow can you find out?	What did you **L**earn?

Prediction _____

Assessment and planning form

Student's name _____ Date of planning _____

Core concept of the lesson _____

	Evidence of learning	Changes needed in instruction to improve learning
Core skill Has the student mastered the core concept? Has the student mastered the vocabulary?		
Functional applications Does the student apply the skill to real-life contexts?		
Conceptual generalization Does the student show understanding of the concept versus repeating a memorized response?		
Inclusion How has the student applied the skill during general education lessons?		
Next steps What is the next step for learning?		

Progress monitoring form

Student's name _____   Date_____

Unit: ☐ Earth   ☐ Biology   ☐ Waters   ☐ Chemistry   Lesson _____

Key: – error   + independent correct   M model/prompt

Dates					
Picture cards					
Word cards					
Picture/word card match					
Concept statement:					

References

Alberto, P. A., & Troutman, A. C. (1999). *Applied behavior analysis for teachers* (5th ed.). Upper Saddle River, NJ: Merrill-Prentice Hall.

Anderson, R. C., Spiro, R. J., & Anderson, M. C. (1978). Schemata as scaffolding for the representation of information in connected discourse. *American Educational Research Journal, 15,* 433–440.

Browder, D. M., & Shear, S. M. (1996). Interspersal of known items in a treatment package to teach sight words to students with behavior disorders. *Journal of Special Education, 29,* 400–413.

Browder, D. M., Spooner, F., Ahlgrim-Delzell, L., Flowers, C., Algozzine, R., & Karvonen, M. (2004). A content analysis of the curricular philosophies reflected in states' alternate assessment performance indicators. *Research and Practice in Severe Disabilities, 28,* 165–181.

Browder, D. M., Spooner, F., Ahlgrim-Delzell, L., Wakeman, S. Y., & Harris, A. (2008). A meta-analysis on teaching mathematics to students with significant cognitive disabilities. *Exceptional Children, 74,* 407–432.

Browder, D. M., Trela, K., Courtade, G. R., Jimenez, B. A., & Knight, V. (2008). *Teaching mathematics and science standards to students with moderate and severe developmental disabilities.* Manuscript submitted for review.

Browder, D. M., Trela, K. C., & Jimenez, B. A. (2007). Training teachers to follow a task analysis to engage middle school students with moderate and severe developmental disabilities in grade-appropriate literature. *Focus on Autism and Other Developmental Disabilities, 22,* 209–219.

Collins, B. (2007). *Moderate and severe disabilities: A foundational approach.* Columbus, OH: Prentice Hall, Merrill.

Courtade, G., Browder, D., Spooner, F., & DiBiase, W. (2008). *The effects of inquiry-based science instruction on teachers of students with significant disabilities.* Manuscript submitted for review.

Courtade, G., Spooner, F., & Browder, D. (2007). A review of studies with students with significant cognitive disabilities that link to science standards. *Research and Practice for Persons with Severe Disabilities, 32,* 43–49.

Doyle, P. M., Gast. D. L., Wolery, M., Ault, M. J., & Farmer, J. A. (1990). Use of constant time delay in small group instruction: A study of observational and incidental learning. *Journal of Special Education, 23,* 369–385.

Erikson, K. A., & Koppenhaver, D. A. (1997). Integrated communication and literacy instruction for a child with multiple disabilities. *Focus on Autism & Other Developmental Disabilities, 12,* 142–151.

Gast, D. L., Winterling, V., Wolery, M., & Farmer, J. A. (1992). Teaching first-aid skills to students with moderate handicaps in small group instruction. *Education & Treatment of Children, 15,* 101–124.

Individuals with Disabilities Education Act (IDEA) Amendments of 1997, PL 105-17, 20 U.S.C. §§ 1400 et seq.

Jimenez, B. A., Browder, D. M., & Courtade, G. (2008). Teaching an algebraic equation to students with moderate disabilities. *Education and Training in Developmental Disabilities, 43,* 266–274.

Magnusson, S. J., & Palincsar, A. S. (1995). The learning environment as a site of science education reform. *Theory into Practice, 34,* 43–50.

Marchand-Martella, N. E., Martella, R. C., Christensen, A. M., Agran, M., & Young, K. R. (1992). Teaching a first aid skill to students with disabilities using two training programs. *Education & Treatment of Children, 15,* 15–31.

National Council of Teachers of Mathematics (NCTM). (2000). *Principles and standards for school mathematics.* Reston, VA: Author.

National Research Council (NRC). (1996). *National science education standards.* Washington, DC: National Academy Press.

No Child Left Behind Act of 2001, Pub. L. No. 107-110, 115 Stat. 1425 (2002).

Schneider, L. S., & Renner, J. W. (1980). Concrete and formal teaching. *Journal of Research in Science Teaching, 17,* 503–517.

Scruggs, T. E., & Mastropieri, M. A. (1995). Science and students with mental retardation: An analysis of curriculum features and learner characteristics. *Science Education, 79,* 251–271.

Shymansky, J. A., Kyle, W. C., Jr., & Alport, J. M. (1983). The effects of new science curricula on student performance. *Journal of Research in Science Teaching, 20,* 387–404.

Spooner, F., Stem, B., & Test, D. W. (1989). Teaching first aid skills to adolescents who are moderately mentally handicapped. *Education and Training in Mental Retardation, 24,* 341–351.

Taber, T. A., Alberto, P. A., Hughes, M., & Seltzer, A. (2002). A strategy for students with moderate disabilities when lost in the community. *Research and Practice for Persons with Severe Disabilities, 27,* 141–152.

Taber, T. A., Alberto, P. A., Seltzer, A., & Hughes, M. (2003). Obtaining assistance when lost in the community using cell phones. *Research and Practice for Persons with Severe Disabilities, 28,* 105–116.

Watson, M., Bain, A., & Houghton, S. (1992). A preliminary study in teaching self-protective skills to children with moderate-to-severe mental retardation. *Journal of Special Education, 26,* 181–194.

Winterling, V., Gast, D. L., Wolery, M., & Farmer, J. A. (1992). Teaching safety skills to high school students with moderate disabilities. *Journal of Applied Behavior Analysis, 25,* 217–227.

Zambo, R. (2005). The power of two: Linking mathematics and literature. *Mathematics Teaching in the Middle School, 10,* 349–399.